ISBN 0-8373-4085-3
C-4085   CAREER EXAMINATION SERIES

This is your
PASSBOOK® for...

Traffic Engineer II

Test Preparation Study Guide
Questions & Answers

NATIONAL LEARNING CORPORATION

(516) 921-8888
(800) 645-6337
FAX: (516) 921-8743
www.passbooks.com
sales @ passbooks.com
info @ passbooks.com

PRINTED IN THE UNITED STATES OF AMERICA

PASSBOOK®
NOTICE

PASSBOOK SERIES®

THE *PASSBOOK SERIES®* has been created to prepare applicants and candidates for the ultimate academic battlefield – the examination room.

At some time in our lives, each and every one of us may be required to take an examination – for validation, matriculation, admission, qualification, registration, certification, or licensure.

Based on the assumption that every applicant or candidate has met the basic formal educational standards, has taken the required number of courses, and read the necessary texts, the *PASSBOOK SERIES®* furnishes the one special preparation which may assure passing with confidence, instead of failing with insecurity. Examination questions – together with answers – are furnished as the basic vehicle for study so that the mysteries of the examination and its compounding difficulties may be eliminated or diminished by a sure method.

This book is meant to help you pass your examination provided that you qualify and are serious in your objective.

The entire field is reviewed through the huge store of content information which is succinctly presented through a provocative and challenging approach – the question-and-answer method.

A climate of success is established by furnishing the correct answers at the end of each test.

You soon learn to recognize types of questions, forms of questions, and patterns of questioning. You may even begin to anticipate expected outcomes.

You perceive that many questions are repeated or adapted so that you can gain acute insights, which may enable you to score many sure points.

You learn how to confront new questions, or types of questions, and to attack them confidently and work out the correct answers.

You note objectives and emphases, and recognize pitfalls and dangers, so that you may make positive educational adjustments.

Moreover, you are kept fully informed in relation to new concepts, methods, practices, and directions in the field.

You discover that you are actually taking the examination all the time: you are preparing for the examination by "taking" an examination, not by reading extraneous and/or supererogatory textbooks.

In short, this PASSBOOK®, used directedly, should be an important factor in helping you to pass your test.

TRAFFIC ENGINEER II

DUTIES

Under general supervision, an employee in this class receives assignments requiring the application of traffic engineering skills and knowledge on various projects. Assignments are received with general instructions, but incumbents use their own judgment and initiative in solution of details. Supervision may be exercised over technical assistants in any phase of the work. Work is checked and reviewed through conferences while in progress and at its conclusion by professional associates and supervisors. Does related work as required.

SCOPE OF THE EXAMINATION

The <u>written test</u> will cover knowledge, skills and/or abilities in such areas as:

1. Engineering plans, specifications and estimates;
2. Supervision;
3. Principles and practices of traffic and transportation engineering;
4. Traffic control devices and regulations, and collection, analysis and presentation of data; and
5. Highway planning, design, safety and laws.

HOW TO TAKE A TEST

I. YOU MUST PASS AN EXAMINATION

A. WHAT EVERY CANDIDATE SHOULD KNOW

Examination applicants often ask us for help in preparing for the written test. What can I study in advance? What kinds of questions will be asked? How will the test be given? How will the papers be graded?

As an applicant for a civil service examination, you may be wondering about some of these things. Our purpose here is to suggest effective methods of advance study and to describe civil service examinations.

Your chances for success on this examination can be increased if you know how to prepare. Those "pre-examination jitters" can be reduced if you know what to expect. You can even experience an adventure in good citizenship if you know why civil service exams are given.

B. WHY ARE CIVIL SERVICE EXAMINATIONS GIVEN?

Civil service examinations are important to you in two ways. As a citizen, you want public jobs filled by employees who know how to do their work. As a job seeker, you want a fair chance to compete for that job on an equal footing with other candidates. The best-known means of accomplishing this two-fold goal is the competitive examination.

Exams are widely publicized throughout the nation. They may be administered for jobs in federal, state, city, municipal, town or village governments or agencies.

Any citizen may apply, with some limitations, such as the age or residence of applicants. Your experience and education may be reviewed to see whether you meet the requirements for the particular examination. When these requirements exist, they are reasonable and applied consistently to all applicants. Thus, a competitive examination may cause you some uneasiness now, but it is your privilege and safeguard.

C. HOW ARE CIVIL SERVICE EXAMS DEVELOPED?

Examinations are carefully written by trained technicians who are specialists in the field known as "psychological measurement," in consultation with recognized authorities in the field of work that the test will cover. These experts recommend the subject matter areas or skills to be tested; only those knowledges or skills important to your success on the job are included. The most reliable books and source materials available are used as references. Together, the experts and technicians judge the difficulty level of the questions.

Test technicians know how to phrase questions so that the problem is clearly stated. Their ethics do not permit "trick" or "catch" questions. Questions may have been tried out on sample groups, or subjected to statistical analysis, to determine their usefulness.

Written tests are often used in combination with performance tests, ratings of training and experience, and oral interviews. All of these measures combine to form the best-known means of finding the right person for the right job.

II. HOW TO PASS THE WRITTEN TEST

A. NATURE OF THE EXAMINATION

To prepare intelligently for civil service examinations, you should know how they differ from school examinations you have taken. In school you were assigned certain definite pages to read or subjects to cover. The examination questions were quite detailed and usually emphasized memory. Civil service exams, on the other hand, try to discover your present ability to perform the duties of a position, plus your potentiality to learn these duties. In other words, a civil service exam attempts to predict how successful you will be. Questions cover such a broad area that they cannot be as minute and detailed as school exam questions.

In the public service similar kinds of work, or positions, are grouped together in one "class." This process is known as *position-classification*. All the positions in a class are paid according to the salary range for that class. One class title covers all of these positions, and they are all tested by the same examination.

B. FOUR BASIC STEPS

1) Study the announcement

How, then, can you know what subjects to study? Our best answer is: "Learn as much as possible about the class of positions for which you've applied." The exam will test the knowledge, skills and abilities needed to do the work.

Your most valuable source of information about the position you want is the official exam announcement. This announcement lists the training and experience qualifications. Check these standards and apply only if you come reasonably close to meeting them.

The brief description of the position in the examination announcement offers some clues to the subjects which will be tested. Think about the job itself. Review the duties in your mind. Can you perform them, or are there some in which you are rusty? Fill in the blank spots in your preparation.

Many jurisdictions preview the written test in the exam announcement by including a section called "Knowledge and Abilities Required," "Scope of the Examination," or some similar heading. Here you will find out specifically what fields will be tested.

2) Review your own background

Once you learn in general what the position is all about, and what you need to know to do the work, ask yourself which subjects you already know fairly well and which need improvement. You may wonder whether to concentrate on improving your strong areas or on building some background in your fields of weakness. When the announcement has specified "some knowledge" or "considerable knowledge," or has used adjectives like "beginning principles of…" or "advanced … methods," you can get a clue as to the number and difficulty of questions to be asked in any given field. More questions, and hence broader coverage, would be included for those subjects which are more important in the work. Now weigh your strengths and weaknesses against the job requirements and prepare accordingly.

3) Determine the level of the position

Another way to tell how intensively you should prepare is to understand the level of the job for which you are applying. Is it the entering level? In other words, is this the position in which beginners in a field of work are hired? Or is it an intermediate or advanced level? Sometimes this is indicated by such words as "Junior" or "Senior" in the class title. Other jurisdictions use Roman numerals to designate the level – Clerk I, Clerk II, for example. The word "Supervisor" sometimes appears in the title. If the level is not indicated by the title, check the description of duties. Will you be working under very close supervision, or will you have responsibility for independent decisions in this work?

4) Choose appropriate study materials

Now that you know the subjects to be examined and the relative amount of each subject to be covered, you can choose suitable study materials. For beginning level jobs, or even advanced ones, if you have a pronounced weakness in some aspect of your training, read a modern, standard textbook in that field. Be sure it is up to date and has general coverage. Such books are normally available at your library, and the librarian will be glad to help you locate one. For entry-level positions, questions of appropriate difficulty are chosen – neither highly advanced questions, nor those too simple. Such questions require careful thought but not advanced training.

If the position for which you are applying is technical or advanced, you will read more advanced, specialized material. If you are already familiar with the basic principles of your field, elementary textbooks would waste your time. Concentrate on advanced textbooks and technical periodicals. Think through the concepts and review difficult problems in your field.

These are all general sources. You can get more ideas on your own initiative, following these leads. For example, training manuals and publications of the government agency which employs workers in your field can be useful, particularly for technical and professional positions. A letter or visit to the government department involved may result in more specific study suggestions, and certainly will provide you with a more definite idea of the exact nature of the position you are seeking.

III. KINDS OF TESTS

Tests are used for purposes other than measuring knowledge and ability to perform specified duties. For some positions, it is equally important to test ability to make adjustments to new situations or to profit from training. In others, basic mental abilities not dependent on information are essential. Questions which test these things may not appear as pertinent to the duties of the position as those which test for knowledge and information. Yet they are often highly important parts of a fair examination. For very general questions, it is almost impossible to help you direct your study efforts. What we can do is to point out some of the more common of these general abilities needed in public service positions and describe some typical questions.

1) General information

Broad, general information has been found useful for predicting job success in some kinds of work. This is tested in a variety of ways, from vocabulary lists to questions about current events. Basic background in some field of work, such as sociology or economics, may be sampled in a group of questions. Often these are principles which have become familiar to most persons through exposure rather than through formal training. It is difficult to advise you how to study for these questions; being alert to the world around you is our best suggestion.

2) Verbal ability

An example of an ability needed in many positions is verbal or language ability. Verbal ability is, in brief, the ability to use and understand words. Vocabulary and grammar tests are typical measures of this ability. Reading comprehension or paragraph interpretation questions are common in many kinds of civil service tests. You are given a paragraph of written material and asked to find its central meaning.

3) Numerical ability

Number skills can be tested by the familiar arithmetic problem, by checking paired lists of numbers to see which are alike and which are different, or by interpreting charts and graphs. In the latter test, a graph may be printed in the test booklet which you are asked to use as the basis for answering questions.

4) Observation

A popular test for law-enforcement positions is the observation test. A picture is shown to you for several minutes, then taken away. Questions about the picture test your ability to observe both details and larger elements.

5) Following directions

In many positions in the public service, the employee must be able to carry out written instructions dependably and accurately. You may be given a chart with several columns, each column listing a variety of information. The questions require you to carry out directions involving the information given in the chart.

6) Skills and aptitudes

Performance tests effectively measure some manual skills and aptitudes. When the skill is one in which you are trained, such as typing or shorthand, you can practice. These tests are often very much like those given in business school or high school courses. For many of the other skills and aptitudes, however, no short-time preparation can be made. Skills and abilities natural to you or that you have developed throughout your lifetime are being tested.

Many of the general questions just described provide all the data needed to answer the questions and ask you to use your reasoning ability to find the answers. Your best preparation for these tests, as well as for tests of facts and ideas, is to be at your physical and mental best. You, no doubt, have your own methods of getting into an exam-taking mood and keeping "in shape." The next section lists some ideas on this subject.

IV. KINDS OF QUESTIONS

Only rarely is the "essay" question, which you answer in narrative form, used in civil service tests. Civil service tests are usually of the short-answer type. Full instructions for answering these questions will be given to you at the examination. But in case this is your first experience with short-answer questions and separate answer sheets, here is what you need to know:

1) Multiple-choice Questions

Most popular of the short-answer questions is the "multiple choice" or "best answer" question. It can be used, for example, to test for factual knowledge, ability to solve problems or judgment in meeting situations found at work.

A multiple-choice question is normally one of three types—

- It can begin with an incomplete statement followed by several possible endings. You are to find the one ending which *best* completes the statement, although some of the others may not be entirely wrong.
- It can also be a complete statement in the form of a question which is answered by choosing one of the statements listed.
- It can be in the form of a problem – again you select the best answer.

Here is an example of a multiple-choice question with a discussion which should give you some clues as to the method for choosing the right answer:

When an employee has a complaint about his assignment, the action which will *best* help him overcome his difficulty is to
- A. discuss his difficulty with his coworkers
- B. take the problem to the head of the organization
- C. take the problem to the person who gave him the assignment
- D. say nothing to anyone about his complaint

In answering this question, you should study each of the choices to find which is best. Consider choice "A" – Certainly an employee may discuss his complaint with fellow employees, but no change or improvement can result, and the complaint remains unresolved. Choice "B" is a poor choice since the head of the organization probably does not know what assignment you have been given, and taking your problem to him is known as "going over the head" of the supervisor. The supervisor, or person who made the assignment, is the person who can clarify it or correct any injustice. Choice "C" is, therefore, correct. To say nothing, as in choice "D," is unwise. Supervisors have and interest in knowing the problems employees are facing, and the employee is seeking a solution to his problem.

2) True/False Questions

The "true/false" or "right/wrong" form of question is sometimes used. Here a complete statement is given. Your job is to decide whether the statement is right or wrong.

SAMPLE: A person-to-person long-distance telephone call costs less than a station-to-station call to the same city.

This statement is wrong, or false, since person-to-person calls are more expensive.

This is not a complete list of all possible question forms, although most of the others are variations of these common types. You will always get complete directions for answering questions. Be sure you understand *how* to mark your answers – ask questions until you do.

V. RECORDING YOUR ANSWERS

For an examination with very few applicants, you may be told to record your answers in the test booklet itself. Separate answer sheets are much more common. If this separate answer sheet is to be scored by machine – and this is often the case – it is highly important that you mark your answers correctly in order to get credit.

An electric scoring machine is often used in civil service offices because of the speed with which papers can be scored. Machine-scored answer sheets must be marked with a pencil, which will be given to you. This pencil has a high graphite content which responds to the electric scoring machine. As a matter of fact, stray dots may register as answers, so do not let your pencil rest on the answer sheet while you are pondering the correct answer. Also, if your pencil lead breaks or is otherwise defective, ask for another.

Since the answer sheet will be dropped in a slot in the scoring machine, be careful not to bend the corners or get the paper crumpled.

The answer sheet normally has five vertical columns of numbers, with 30 numbers to a column. These numbers correspond to the question numbers in your test booklet. After each number, going across the page are four or five pairs of dotted lines. These short dotted lines have small letters or numbers above them. The first two pairs may also have a "T" or "F" above the letters. This indicates that the first two pairs only are to be used if the questions are of the true-false type. If the questions are multiple choice, disregard the "T" and "F" and pay attention only to the small letters or numbers.

Answer your questions in the manner of the sample that follows:

32. The largest city in the United States is
   A. Washington, D.C.
   B. New York City
   C. Chicago
   D. Detroit
   E. San Francisco

1) Choose the answer you think is best. (New York City is the largest, so "B" is correct.)
2) Find the row of dotted lines numbered the same as the question you are answering. (Find row number 32)
3) Find the pair of dotted lines corresponding to the answer. (Find the pair of lines under the mark "B.")
4) Make a solid black mark between the dotted lines.

VI. BEFORE THE TEST

Common sense will help you find procedures to follow to get ready for an examination. Too many of us, however, overlook these sensible measures. Indeed, nervousness and fatigue have been found to be the most serious reasons why applicants fail to do their best on civil service tests. Here is a list of reminders:

- Begin your preparation early – Don't wait until the last minute to go scurrying around for books and materials or to find out what the position is all about.
- Prepare continuously – An hour a night for a week is better than an all-night cram session. This has been definitely established. What is more, a night a

week for a month will return better dividends than crowding your study into a shorter period of time.

- Locate the place of the exam – You have been sent a notice telling you when and where to report for the examination. If the location is in a different town or otherwise unfamiliar to you, it would be well to inquire the best route and learn something about the building.
- Relax the night before the test – Allow your mind to rest. Do not study at all that night. Plan some mild recreation or diversion; then go to bed early and get a good night's sleep.
- Get up early enough to make a leisurely trip to the place for the test – This way unforeseen events, traffic snarls, unfamiliar buildings, etc. will not upset you.
- Dress comfortably – A written test is not a fashion show. You will be known by number and not by name, so wear something comfortable.
- Leave excess paraphernalia at home – Shopping bags and odd bundles will get in your way. You need bring only the items mentioned in the official notice you received; usually everything you need is provided. Do not bring reference books to the exam. They will only confuse those last minutes and be taken away from you when in the test room.
- Arrive somewhat ahead of time – If because of transportation schedules you must get there very early, bring a newspaper or magazine to take your mind off yourself while waiting.
- Locate the examination room – When you have found the proper room, you will be directed to the seat or part of the room where you will sit. Sometimes you are given a sheet of instructions to read while you are waiting. Do not fill out any forms until you are told to do so; just read them and be prepared.
- Relax and prepare to listen to the instructions
- If you have any physical problem that may keep you from doing your best, be sure to tell the test administrator. If you are sick or in poor health, you really cannot do your best on the exam. You can come back and take the test some other time.

VII. AT THE TEST

The day of the test is here and you have the test booklet in your hand. The temptation to get going is very strong. Caution! There is more to success than knowing the right answers. You must know how to identify your papers and understand variations in the type of short-answer question used in this particular examination. Follow these suggestions for maximum results from your efforts:

1) Cooperate with the monitor

The test administrator has a duty to create a situation in which you can be as much at ease as possible. He will give instructions, tell you when to begin, check to see that you are marking your answer sheet correctly, and so on. He is not there to guard you, although he will see that your competitors do not take unfair advantage. He wants to help you do your best.

2) Listen to all instructions

Don't jump the gun! Wait until you understand all directions. In most civil service tests you get more time than you need to answer the questions. So don't be in a hurry.

Read each word of instructions until you clearly understand the meaning. Study the examples, listen to all announcements and follow directions. Ask questions if you do not understand what to do.

3) Identify your papers

Civil service exams are usually identified by number only. You will be assigned a number; you must not put your name on your test papers. Be sure to copy your number correctly. Since more than one exam may be given, copy your exact examination title.

4) Plan your time

Unless you are told that a test is a "speed" or "rate of work" test, speed itself is usually not important. Time enough to answer all the questions will be provided, but this does not mean that you have all day. An overall time limit has been set. Divide the total time (in minutes) by the number of questions to determine the approximate time you have for each question.

5) Do not linger over difficult questions

If you come across a difficult question, mark it with a paper clip (useful to have along) and come back to it when you have been through the booklet. One caution if you do this – be sure to skip a number on your answer sheet as well. Check often to be sure that you have not lost your place and that you are marking in the row numbered the same as the question you are answering.

6) Read the questions

Be sure you know what the question asks! Many capable people are unsuccessful because they failed to *read* the questions correctly.

7) Answer all questions

Unless you have been instructed that a penalty will be deducted for incorrect answers, it is better to guess than to omit a question.

8) Speed tests

It is often better NOT to guess on speed tests. It has been found that on timed tests people are tempted to spend the last few seconds before time is called in marking answers at random – without even reading them – in the hope of picking up a few extra points. To discourage this practice, the instructions may warn you that your score will be "corrected" for guessing. That is, a penalty will be applied. The incorrect answers will be deducted from the correct ones, or some other penalty formula will be used.

9) Review your answers

If you finish before time is called, go back to the questions you guessed or omitted to give them further thought. Review other answers if you have time.

10) Return your test materials

If you are ready to leave before others have finished or time is called, take ALL your materials to the monitor and leave quietly. Never take any test material with you. The monitor can discover whose papers are not complete, and taking a test booklet may be grounds for disqualification.

VIII. EXAMINATION TECHNIQUES

1) Read the general instructions carefully. These are usually printed on the first page of the exam booklet. As a rule, these instructions refer to the timing of the examination; the fact that you should not start work until the signal and must stop work at a signal, etc. If there are any *special* instructions, such as a choice of questions to be answered, make sure that you note this instruction carefully.

2) When you are ready to start work on the examination, that is as soon as the signal has been given, read the instructions to each question booklet, underline any key words or phrases, such as *least, best, outline, describe* and the like. In this way you will tend to answer as requested rather than discover on reviewing your paper that you *listed without describing*, that you selected the *worst* choice rather than the *best* choice, etc.

3) If the examination is of the objective or multiple-choice type – that is, each question will also give a series of possible answers: A, B, C or D, and you are called upon to select the best answer and write the letter next to that answer on your answer paper – it is advisable to start answering each question in turn. There may be anywhere from 50 to 100 such questions in the three or four hours allotted and you can see how much time would be taken if you read through all the questions before beginning to answer any. Furthermore, if you come across a question or group of questions which you know would be difficult to answer, it would undoubtedly affect your handling of all the other questions.

4) If the examination is of the essay type and contains but a few questions, it is a moot point as to whether you should read all the questions before starting to answer any one. Of course, if you are given a choice – say five out of seven and the like – then it is essential to read all the questions so you can eliminate the two that are most difficult. If, however, you are asked to answer all the questions, there may be danger in trying to answer the easiest one first because you may find that you will spend too much time on it. The best technique is to answer the first question, then proceed to the second, etc.

5) Time your answers. Before the exam begins, write down the time it started, then add the time allowed for the examination and write down the time it must be completed, then divide the time available somewhat as follows:
   - If 3-1/2 hours are allowed, that would be 210 minutes. If you have 80 objective-type questions, that would be an average of 2-1/2 minutes per question. Allow yourself no more than 2 minutes per question, or a total of 160 minutes, which will permit about 50 minutes to review.
   - If for the time allotment of 210 minutes there are 7 essay questions to answer, that would average about 30 minutes a question. Give yourself only 25 minutes per question so that you have about 35 minutes to review.

6) The most important instruction is to *read each question* and make sure you know what is wanted. The second most important instruction is to *time yourself properly* so that you answer every question. The third most

important instruction is to *answer every question*. Guess if you have to but include something for each question. Remember that you will receive no credit for a blank and will probably receive some credit if you write something in answer to an essay question. If you guess a letter – say "B" for a multiple-choice question – you may have guessed right. If you leave a blank as an answer to a multiple-choice question, the examiners may respect your feelings but it will not add a point to your score. Some exams may penalize you for wrong answers, so in such cases *only*, you may not want to guess unless you have some basis for your answer.

7) Suggestions
   a. Objective-type questions
      1. Examine the question booklet for proper sequence of pages and questions
      2. Read all instructions carefully
      3. Skip any question which seems too difficult; return to it after all other questions have been answered
      4. Apportion your time properly; do not spend too much time on any single question or group of questions
      5. Note and underline key words – *all, most, fewest, least, best, worst, same, opposite*, etc.
      6. Pay particular attention to negatives
      7. Note unusual option, e.g., unduly long, short, complex, different or similar in content to the body of the question
      8. Observe the use of "hedging" words – *probably, may, most likely*, etc.
      9. Make sure that your answer is put next to the same number as the question
      10. Do not second-guess unless you have good reason to believe the second answer is definitely more correct
      11. Cross out original answer if you decide another answer is more accurate; do not erase until you are ready to hand your paper in
      12. Answer all questions; guess unless instructed otherwise
      13. Leave time for review

   b. Essay questions
      1. Read each question carefully
      2. Determine exactly what is wanted. Underline key words or phrases.
      3. Decide on outline or paragraph answer
      4. Include many different points and elements unless asked to develop any one or two points or elements
      5. Show impartiality by giving pros and cons unless directed to select one side only
      6. Make and write down any assumptions you find necessary to answer the questions
      7. Watch your English, grammar, punctuation and choice of words
      8. Time your answers; don't crowd material

8) Answering the essay question

Most essay questions can be answered by framing the specific response around several key words or ideas. Here are a few such key words or ideas:

M's: manpower, materials, methods, money, management
P's: purpose, program, policy, plan, procedure, practice, problems, pitfalls, personnel, public relations

    a. Six basic steps in handling problems:
1. Preliminary plan and background development
2. Collect information, data and facts
3. Analyze and interpret information, data and facts
4. Analyze and develop solutions as well as make recommendations
5. Prepare report and sell recommendations
6. Install recommendations and follow up effectiveness

    b. Pitfalls to avoid
1. *Taking things for granted* – A statement of the situation does not necessarily imply that each of the elements is necessarily true; for example, a complaint may be invalid and biased so that all that can be taken for granted is that a complaint has been registered
2. *Considering only one side of a situation* – Wherever possible, indicate several alternatives and then point out the reasons you selected the best one
3. *Failing to indicate follow up* – Whenever your answer indicates action on your part, make certain that you will take proper follow-up action to see how successful your recommendations, procedures or actions turn out to be
4. *Taking too long in answering any single question* – Remember to time your answers properly

IX. AFTER THE TEST

Scoring procedures differ in detail among civil service jurisdictions although the general principles are the same. Whether the papers are hand-scored or graded by machine we have described, they are nearly always graded by number. That is, the person who marks the paper knows only the number – never the name – of the applicant. Not until all the papers have been graded will they be matched with names. If other tests, such as training and experience or oral interview ratings have been given, scores will be combined. Different parts of the examination usually have different weights. For example, the written test might count 60 percent of the final grade, and a rating of training and experience 40 percent. In many jurisdictions, veterans will have a certain number of points added to their grades.

After the final grade has been determined, the names are placed in grade order and an eligible list is established. There are various methods for resolving ties between those who get the same final grade – probably the most common is to place first the name of the person whose application was received first. Job offers are made from the eligible list in the order the names appear on it. You will be notified of your grade and your rank as soon as all these computations have been made. This will be done as rapidly as possible.

People who are found to meet the requirements in the announcement are called "eligibles." Their names are put on a list of eligible candidates. An eligible's chances of getting a job depend on how high he stands on this list and how fast agencies are filling jobs from the list.

When a job is to be filled from a list of eligibles, the agency asks for the names of people on the list of eligibles for that job. When the civil service commission receives this request, it sends to the agency the names of the three people highest on this list. Or, if the job to be filled has specialized requirements, the office sends the agency the names of the top three persons who meet these requirements from the general list.

The appointing officer makes a choice from among the three people whose names were sent to him. If the selected person accepts the appointment, the names of the others are put back on the list to be considered for future openings.

That is the rule in hiring from all kinds of eligible lists, whether they are for typist, carpenter, chemist, or something else. For every vacancy, the appointing officer has his choice of any one of the top three eligibles on the list. This explains why the person whose name is on top of the list sometimes does not get an appointment when some of the persons lower on the list do. If the appointing officer chooses the second or third eligible, the No. 1 eligible does not get a job at once, but stays on the list until he is appointed or the list is terminated.

X. HOW TO PASS THE INTERVIEW TEST

The examination for which you applied requires an oral interview test. You have already taken the written test and you are now being called for the interview test – the final part of the formal examination.

You may think that it is not possible to prepare for an interview test and that there are no procedures to follow during an interview. Our purpose is to point out some things you can do in advance that will help you and some good rules to follow and pitfalls to avoid while you are being interviewed.

What is an interview supposed to test?

The written examination is designed to test the technical knowledge and competence of the candidate; the oral is designed to evaluate intangible qualities, not readily measured otherwise, and to establish a list showing the relative fitness of each candidate – as measured against his competitors – for the position sought. Scoring is not on the basis of "right" and "wrong," but on a sliding scale of values ranging from "not passable" to "outstanding." As a matter of fact, it is possible to achieve a relatively low score without a single "incorrect" answer because of evident weakness in the qualities being measured.

Occasionally, an examination may consist entirely of an oral test – either an individual or a group oral. In such cases, information is sought concerning the technical knowledges and abilities of the candidate, since there has been no written examination for this purpose. More commonly, however, an oral test is used to supplement a written examination.

Who conducts interviews?

The composition of oral boards varies among different jurisdictions. In nearly all, a representative of the personnel department serves as chairman. One of the members of the board may be a representative of the department in which the candidate would work. In some cases, "outside experts" are used, and, frequently, a businessman or some other representative of the general public is asked to serve. Labor and management or other special groups may be represented. The aim is to secure the services of experts in the appropriate field.

However the board is composed, it is a good idea (and not at all improper or unethical) to ascertain in advance of the interview who the members are and what groups they represent. When you are introduced to them, you will have some idea of their backgrounds and interests, and at least you will not stutter and stammer over their names.

What should be done before the interview?

While knowledge about the board members is useful and takes some of the surprise element out of the interview, there is other preparation which is more substantive. It *is* possible to prepare for an oral interview – in several ways:

1) Keep a copy of your application and review it carefully before the interview

This may be the only document before the oral board, and the starting point of the interview. Know what education and experience you have listed there, and the sequence and dates of all of it. Sometimes the board will ask you to review the highlights of your experience for them; you should not have to hem and haw doing it.

2) Study the class specification and the examination announcement

Usually, the oral board has one or both of these to guide them. The qualities, characteristics or knowledges required by the position sought are stated in these documents. They offer valuable clues as to the nature of the oral interview. For example, if the job involves supervisory responsibilities, the announcement will usually indicate that knowledge of modern supervisory methods and the qualifications of the candidate as a supervisor will be tested. If so, you can expect such questions, frequently in the form of a hypothetical situation which you are expected to solve. NEVER go into an oral without knowledge of the duties and responsibilities of the job you seek.

3) Think through each qualification required

Try to visualize the kind of questions you would ask if you were a board member. How well could you answer them? Try especially to appraise your own knowledge and background in each area, *measured against the job sought*, and identify any areas in which you are weak. Be critical and realistic – do not flatter yourself.

4) Do some general reading in areas in which you feel you may be weak

For example, if the job involves supervision and your past experience has NOT, some general reading in supervisory methods and practices, particularly in the field of human relations, might be useful. Do NOT study agency procedures or detailed manuals. The oral board will be testing your understanding and capacity, not your memory.

5) Get a good night's sleep and watch your general health and mental attitude

You will want a clear head at the interview. Take care of a cold or any other minor ailment, and of course, no hangovers.

What should be done on the day of the interview?

Now comes the day of the interview itself. Give yourself plenty of time to get there. Plan to arrive somewhat ahead of the scheduled time, particularly if your appointment is in the fore part of the day. If a previous candidate fails to appear, the board might be ready for you a bit early. By early afternoon an oral board is almost invariably behind schedule if there are many candidates, and you may have to wait.

Take along a book or magazine to read, or your application to review, but leave any extraneous material in the waiting room when you go in for your interview. In any event, relax and compose yourself.

The matter of dress is important. The board is forming impressions about you – from your experience, your manners, your attitude, and your appearance. Give your personal appearance careful attention. Dress your best, but not your flashiest. Choose conservative, appropriate clothing, and be sure it is immaculate. This is a business interview, and your appearance should indicate that you regard it as such. Besides, being well groomed and properly dressed will help boost your confidence.

Sooner or later, someone will call your name and escort you into the interview room. *This is it.* From here on you are on your own. It is too late for any more preparation. But remember, you asked for this opportunity to prove your fitness, and you are here because your request was granted.

What happens when you go in?

The usual sequence of events will be as follows: The clerk (who is often the board stenographer) will introduce you to the chairman of the oral board, who will introduce you to the other members of the board. Acknowledge the introductions before you sit down. Do not be surprised if you find a microphone facing you or a stenotypist sitting by. Oral interviews are usually recorded in the event of an appeal or other review.

Usually the chairman of the board will open the interview by reviewing the highlights of your education and work experience from your application – primarily for the benefit of the other members of the board, as well as to get the material into the record. Do not interrupt or comment unless there is an error or significant misinterpretation; if that is the case, do not hesitate. But do not quibble about insignificant matters. Also, he will usually ask you some question about your education, experience or your present job – partly to get you to start talking and to establish the interviewing "rapport." He may start the actual questioning, or turn it over to one of the other members. Frequently, each member undertakes the questioning on a particular area, one in which he is perhaps most competent, so you can expect each member to participate in the examination. Because time is limited, you may also expect some rather abrupt switches in the direction the questioning takes, so do not be upset by it. Normally, a board member will not pursue a single line of questioning unless he discovers a particular strength or weakness.

After each member has participated, the chairman will usually ask whether any member has any further questions, then will ask you if you have anything you wish to add. Unless you are expecting this question, it may floor you. Worse, it may start you off on an extended, extemporaneous speech. The board is not usually seeking more information. The question is principally to offer you a last opportunity to present further qualifications or to indicate that you have nothing to add. So, if you feel that a significant qualification or characteristic has been overlooked, it is proper to point it out in a sentence or so. Do not compliment the board on the thoroughness of their examination – they have been sketchy, and you know it. If you wish, merely say, "No thank you, I have nothing further to add." This is a point where you can "talk yourself out" of a good impression or fail to present an important bit of information. Remember, *you close the interview yourself.*

The chairman will then say, "That is all, Mr. _____, thank you." Do not be startled; the interview is over, and quicker than you think. Thank him, gather your belongings and take your leave. Save your sigh of relief for the other side of the door.

How to put your best foot forward

Throughout this entire process, you may feel that the board individually and collectively is trying to pierce your defenses, seek out your hidden weaknesses and embarrass and confuse you. Actually, this is not true. They are obliged to make an appraisal of your qualifications for the job you are seeking, and they want to see you in your best light. Remember, they must interview all candidates and a non-cooperative candidate may become a failure in spite of their best efforts to bring out his qualifications. Here are 15 suggestions that will help you:

1) Be natural – Keep your attitude confident, not cocky

If you are not confident that you can do the job, do not expect the board to be. Do not apologize for your weaknesses, try to bring out your strong points. The board is interested in a positive, not negative, presentation. Cockiness will antagonize any board member and make him wonder if you are covering up a weakness by a false show of strength.

2) Get comfortable, but don't lounge or sprawl

Sit erectly but not stiffly. A careless posture may lead the board to conclude that you are careless in other things, or at least that you are not impressed by the importance of the occasion. Either conclusion is natural, even if incorrect. Do not fuss with your clothing, a pencil or an ashtray. Your hands may occasionally be useful to emphasize a point; do not let them become a point of distraction.

3) Do not wisecrack or make small talk

This is a serious situation, and your attitude should show that you consider it as such. Further, the time of the board is limited – they do not want to waste it, and neither should you.

4) Do not exaggerate your experience or abilities

In the first place, from information in the application or other interviews and sources, the board may know more about you than you think. Secondly, you probably will not get away with it. An experienced board is rather adept at spotting such a situation, so do not take the chance.

5) If you know a board member, do not make a point of it, yet do not hide it

Certainly you are not fooling him, and probably not the other members of the board. Do not try to take advantage of your acquaintanceship – it will probably do you little good.

6) Do not dominate the interview

Let the board do that. They will give you the clues – do not assume that you have to do all the talking. Realize that the board has a number of questions to ask you, and do not try to take up all the interview time by showing off your extensive knowledge of the answer to the first one.

7) Be attentive

You only have 20 minutes or so, and you should keep your attention at its sharpest throughout. When a member is addressing a problem or question to you, give him your undivided attention. Address your reply principally to him, but do not exclude the other board members.

8) Do not interrupt

A board member may be stating a problem for you to analyze. He will ask you a question when the time comes. Let him state the problem, and wait for the question.

9) Make sure you understand the question

Do not try to answer until you are sure what the question is. If it is not clear, restate it in your own words or ask the board member to clarify it for you. However, do not haggle about minor elements.

10) Reply promptly but not hastily

A common entry on oral board rating sheets is "candidate responded readily," or "candidate hesitated in replies." Respond as promptly and quickly as you can, but do not jump to a hasty, ill-considered answer.

11) Do not be peremptory in your answers

A brief answer is proper – but do not fire your answer back. That is a losing game from your point of view. The board member can probably ask questions much faster than you can answer them.

12) Do not try to create the answer you think the board member wants

He is interested in what kind of mind you have and how it works – not in playing games. Furthermore, he can usually spot this practice and will actually grade you down on it.

13) Do not switch sides in your reply merely to agree with a board member

Frequently, a member will take a contrary position merely to draw you out and to see if you are willing and able to defend your point of view. Do not start a debate, yet do not surrender a good position. If a position is worth taking, it is worth defending.

14) Do not be afraid to admit an error in judgment if you are shown to be wrong

The board knows that you are forced to reply without any opportunity for careful consideration. Your answer may be demonstrably wrong. If so, admit it and get on with the interview.

15) Do not dwell at length on your present job

The opening question may relate to your present assignment. Answer the question but do not go into an extended discussion. You are being examined for a *new* job, not your present one. As a matter of fact, try to phrase ALL your answers in terms of the job for which you are being examined.

Basis of Rating

Probably you will forget most of these "do's" and "don'ts" when you walk into the oral interview room. Even remembering them all will not ensure you a passing grade. Perhaps you did not have the qualifications in the first place. But remembering them will help you to put your best foot forward, without treading on the toes of the board members.

Rumor and popular opinion to the contrary notwithstanding, an oral board wants you to make the best appearance possible. They know you are under pressure – but they also want to see how you respond to it as a guide to what your reaction would be under the pressures of the job you seek. They will be influenced by the degree of poise you display, the personal traits you show and the manner in which you respond.

EXAMINATION SECTION

EXAMINATION SECTION
TEST 1

DIRECTIONS: Each question or incomplete statement is followed by several suggested answers or completions. Select the one that BEST answers the question or completes the statement. *PRINT THE LETTER OF THE CORRECT ANSWER IN THE SPACE AT THE RIGHT.*

1. What is represented by the architectural symbol shown at the right?
   - A. Stone concrete
   - B. Cinder concrete
   - C. Gravel
   - D. Plaster

   1.___

2. Poured installation of fiberglass or mineral wool insulation material will typically occur at a rate of _____ cubic feet per day.
   - A. 20
   - B. 80
   - C. 120
   - D. 180

   2.___

3. What is the MOST effective method for backfilling excavated material?
   - A. Sheepfoot roller
   - B. Bulldozer
   - C. Shoveling
   - D. Pneumatic tamper

   3.___

4. Approximately how many square feet of unfinished plank flooring can be installed in an average work day?
   - A. 50
   - B. 150
   - C. 225
   - D. 300

   4.___

5. Studs for concrete basement forms are typically spaced _____ apart.
   - A. 18 inches
   - B. 2 feet
   - C. 4 feet
   - D. 8 feet

   5.___

6. Most construction stone is calculated and purchased by the
   - A. square foot
   - B. linear foot
   - C. cubic yard
   - D. ton

   6.___

7. When earth backfill is replaced at a site, it is required to be compacted to within _____% of the original density.
   - A. 65-75
   - B. 75-90
   - C. 85-95
   - D. 80-100

   7.___

8. What type of brick masonry unit is represented by the drawing shown at the right?
   - A. Norman
   - B. Norwegian
   - C. Corner
   - D. Skippy

   8.___

9. A laborer on a plain gable roof will typically install approximately _____ bundles of straight shingles in an average work day.
   - A. 3-5
   - B. 6-9
   - C. 10-15
   - D. 17-20

   9.___

10. What material is applied behind wall support mesh to
    reduce plaster waste?
    A. Mastic   B. Gypsum board
    C. Chicken wire   D. Asphalt-saturated felt

10.___

11. A _____ line is represented by the mechanical —--
    symbol shown at the right.
    A. fuel oil   B. vent
    C. cold water   D. hot water

11.___

12. Approximately how many square feet of exterior surface
    can be prepared for paint or stain in one hour?
    A. 50   B. 100   C. 150   D. 250

12.___

13. What tool is used to rough level concrete when it is
    still plastic?
    A. Drum   B. Header   C. Float   D. Screed

13.___

14. Most stains that are applied to heavy timber can cover
    about _____ square feet per gallon.
    A. 100   B. 250   C. 350   D. 550

14.___

15. Which of the following is NOT one of the three standard
    methods for installing glazed tile?
    A. Furan resin grout   B. Full mortar beds
    C. Organic adhesives   D. Dry-set thin cement

15.___

16. Generally, the cost for a buildings's heating/air
    conditioning make up about _____% of the total construc-
    tion cost.
    A. 1-3   B. 4-8   C. 5-10   D. 8-12

16.___

17. What is represented by the electrical symbol
    shown at the right?
    A. Lock or key switch
    B. Two-way switch
    C. Switch with duplex receptacle
    D. Triplex receptacle

17.___

18. Most structural lumber is considered *yard dry* at a
    MAXIMUM of about _____% moisture content.
    A. 5   B. 10   C. 20   D. 30

18.___

19. What is the term for a wood or metal edge applied to the
    wall and used as a guide to determine the depth of
    plaster?
    A. Rake   B. Float   C. Screed   D. Stud

19.___

20. Approximately how many single rolls of wall covering
    can be hung by one worker in a typical work day?
    A. 12   B. 20   C. 30   D. 45

20.___

21. What is represented by the architectural symbol shown at the right? 21.____
    A. Structural tile   B. Concrete block
    C. Fire brick   D. Brick

22. Approximately how many square feet of interior wall space can one painter, using a roller, cover in an hour? 22.____
    A. 25-50   B. 100   C. 175-200   D. 250

23. Cement plaster scratch coat for tile installation can typically be applied at a rate of _____ square yards per work day. 23.____
    A. 150   B. 300   C. 500   D. 750

24. MOST gas lines are made of 24.____
    A. black iron   B. copper
    C. galvanized steel   D. plastic

25. For most types of resilient flooring installation, approximately how many hours of labor will be required to install 100 square feet? 25.____
    A. $\frac{1}{2}$ B. 1   C. 3   D. $4\frac{1}{2}$

KEY (CORRECT ANSWERS)

1. C		11. C	
2. A		12. B	
3. B		13. C	
4. B		14. B	
5. C		15. A	
6. D		16. B	
7. C		17. C	
8. A		18. C	
9. C		19. C	
10. D		20. C	

21. C
22. C
23. B
24. A
25. C

TEST 2

DIRECTIONS: Each question or incomplete statement is followed by several suggested answers or completions. Select the one that BEST answers the question or completes the statement. *PRINT THE LETTER OF THE CORRECT ANSWER IN THE SPACE AT THE RIGHT.*

1. Approximately how much labor will be required for the testing of a single unit of installed water or sewer line? 1.___
   A. 30 minutes B. 1 hour
   C. 2 hours D. 3 hours

2. Concrete reinforcing bars are sized according to ____ inch increments. 2.___
   A. 1/16 B. 1/8 C. 1/4 D. 1/2

3. Approximately how many square feet of 4¼" x 4¼" glazed wall tile, set in mortar, can be applied in an average work day? 3.___
   A. 60 B. 130 C. 175 D. 220

4. In residential work, what type of estimate is MOST likely to be used to estimate the cost of excavation work? 4.___
   A. Quantity survey
   B. Lump-sum amount
   C. Cost-per-square-foot estimate
   D. Unit cost estimate

5. What type of brick masonry unit is represented by the drawing shown at the right? 5.___
   A. Trough
   B. Economy
   C. King Norman
   D. Engineer

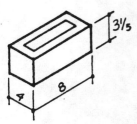

6. Which of the following types of windows would be MOST expensive to install? 6.___
   A. Aluminum, single-hung vertical
   B. Wood, double-hung
   C. Steel, projected vent
   D. Aluminum, projected vent

7. For estimating the labor cost of the installation of tile base and cap units, the typical tile labor time should be multiplied by 7.___
   A. ½ B. 2 C. 3 D. 4

8. What is represented by the architectural symbol shown at the right? 8.___
   A. Plywood
   C. Brick
   B. Vertical paneling
   D. Rough lumber

9. Approximately how long should it take a 2-person crew to install 100 linear feet of 4" x 6" girder?
   A. 30 minutes
   B. 1 hour
   C. 3 hours
   D. 1 work day

9.___

10. Each of the following is considered a fixed overhead cost EXCEPT
    A. office rent
    B. job site utilities
    C. assembly space
    D. stationery

10.___

11. How many square feet of solid plywood roof sheathing should two carpenters be able to install in a typical work day?
    A. 400   B. 800   C. 1,000   D. 1,400

11.___

12. What type of concrete masonry unit is represented by the drawing shown at the right?
    A. Floor
    B. Bull nose
    C. Trough
    D. Jamb

12.___

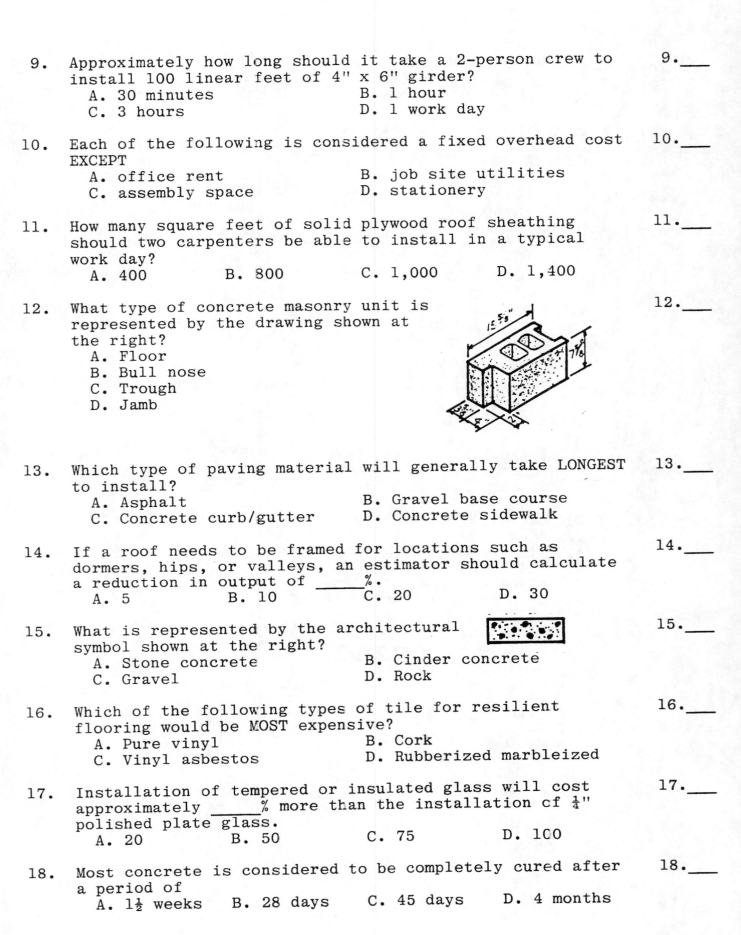

13. Which type of paving material will generally take LONGEST to install?
    A. Asphalt
    B. Gravel base course
    C. Concrete curb/gutter
    D. Concrete sidewalk

13.___

14. If a roof needs to be framed for locations such as dormers, hips, or valleys, an estimator should calculate a reduction in output of _____%.
    A. 5   B. 10   C. 20   D. 30

14.___

15. What is represented by the architectural symbol shown at the right?
    A. Stone concrete
    B. Cinder concrete
    C. Gravel
    D. Rock

15.___

16. Which of the following types of tile for resilient flooring would be MOST expensive?
    A. Pure vinyl
    B. Cork
    C. Vinyl asbestos
    D. Rubberized marbleized

16.___

17. Installation of tempered or insulated glass will cost approximately _____% more than the installation of ¼" polished plate glass.
    A. 20   B. 50   C. 75   D. 100

17.___

18. Most concrete is considered to be completely cured after a period of
    A. 1½ weeks   B. 28 days   C. 45 days   D. 4 months

18.___

19. What type of window is hinged at the top so that it may be opened outward at the bottom?
    A. Storm   B. Casement   C. Sash   D. Awning

20. What is the usual thickness, in inches, for the finish coat in MOST plastering projects?
    A. 1/16   B. 1/8   C. 1/4   D. 1/2

21. Due to the *swell factor* involved in excavation, 1 cubic yard of excavated sand or gravel may measure _____ % more as waste or backfill.
    A. 10   B. 20   C. 30   D. 50

22. What is represented by the electrical symbol shown at the right?
    A. Blanked outlet
    B. Signal push button
    C. Special purpose outlet
    D. Gauge

23. What type of nails are typically used for installing rafters?
    A. 4d   B. 8d   C. 12d   D. 16d

24. Most flat interior paint averages a coverage of about _____ square feet per gallon.
    A. 100-150   B. 200-250   C. 300-400   D. 450-550

25. Which of the following types of doors would be MOST expensive?
    A. Hollow core, birch-veneer face
    B. Solid core, walnut-faced
    C. Hollow core, hardboard-faced
    D. Solid core, birch-veneer face

KEY (CORRECT ANSWERS)

1. C	11. D
2. B	12. D
3. A	13. C
4. D	14. B
5. D	15. A
6. B	16. A
7. B	17. D
8. D	18. B
9. C	19. D
10. B	20. B

21. B
22. C
23. D
24. C
25. B

TEST 3

DIRECTIONS: Each question or incomplete statement is followed by several suggested answers or completions. Select the one that BEST answers the question or completes the statement. *PRINT THE LETTER OF THE CORRECT ANSWER IN THE SPACE AT THE RIGHT.*

1. Most tubs, toilets, sinks, and lavatories require an average of _____ hours labor for the installation of finish plumbing.
   A. 3   B. 5   C. 7   D. 9

   1._____

2. What size is most wire used for ranges and other heavy-draw equipment?
   A. 2-4   B. 5-7   C. 8-10   D. 12-16

   2._____

3. A 4-man crew using hand application will typically be able to apply _____ square yards of gypsum plaster in one work day.
   A. 35-40   B. 45-60   C. 75-80   D. 85-100

   3._____

4. A _____ is represented by the mechanical symbol shown at the right.
   A. lock and shield valve   B. strainer
   C. pressure reducing valve   D. drain line

   4._____

5. What type of drywall surface is used for ceramic tile installation?
   A. Plain manila paper   B. Chemically-treated paper
   C. Aluminum foil   D. Greenboard

   5._____

6. Which of the following steps in a grading-quantity estimation would be performed LAST?
   A. Determine approximate finish grade
   B. Calculate difference between cut and fill
   C. Estimate elevation of grid corners from contours
   D. Average the elevation of each grid square

   6._____

7. In order to give desired rigidity to a wall, the top plates must overlap AT LEAST _____ inches at each joint along the wall.
   A. 12   B. 24   C. 48   D. 60

   7._____

8. The horizontal framing member above window and door openings is called the
   A. molding   B. footer   C. chord   D. lintel

   8._____

9. Which of the following waterproofing materials is MOST expensive?
   A. 30-lb. asphalt paper with elastic adhesive
   B. Elastomeric waterproofing (1/32")
   C. Asphalt-coated protective board, installed in mastic
   D. Sprayed-on bituminous coating

   9._____

10. If a site lawn is seeded, for how long will a contractor typically assume the responsibility for maintaining the lawn?
    A. 3 weeks   B. 1 month   C. 3 months   D. 6 months

     10.___

11. What is represented by the architectural symbol shown at the right?
    A. Brick   B. Vertical paneling
    C. Ceramic tile   D. Concrete block

     11.___

12. In an average work day, approximately how many square feet of brick (on sand bed) paving can be laid down?
    A. 80-100   B. 600   C. 1800   D. 3000-4000

     12.___

13. In lumber take-off and ordering, costs are kept separate and calculated for each of the following specifications EXCEPT
    A. size   B. grade   C. length   D. species

     13.___

14. The excavation of sand will require an angle of repose (slope) of 1 ft. vertical to _____ ft. horizontal.
    A. 3/4   B. 1   C. $1\frac{1}{2}$ D. 2

     14.___

15. Concrete sidewalks are typically poured to a depth of _____ inches.
    A. 2   B. 4   C. 6   D. 8

     15.___

16. What type of concrete masonry unit is represented by the drawing shown at the right?
    A. Stretcher
    B. Pier
    C. Jamb
    D. Beam

     16.___

17. Each of the following is a factor in estimating the total cost according to a quantity survey EXCEPT
    A. quantity of each material
    B. square foot area of building
    C. cost of labor for each unit of material
    D. profit

     17.___

18. Approximately how many hours will it take carpentry labor to install 100 square feet of wall space, without openings?
    A. 1   B. 3   C. 5   D. 7

     18.___

19. Each of the following is included in a site plan EXCEPT
    A. size of property
    B. legal description
    C. number of external doors
    D. driveways

     19.___

20. What is represented by the electrical symbol shown at the right?
    20.___
    A. Street light and bracket
    B. Call system
    C. Wall bracket light fixture
    D. Sound system

21. Normally, horizontal reinforcements for masonry walls are spaced about _____ inches apart.
    21.___
    A. 18   B. 36   C. 48   D. 60

22. Which of the following paving materials is generally LEAST expensive?
    22.___
    A. Brick on sand bed   B. Random flagstone
    C. Asphalt   D. Concrete

23. What type of nails are typically used for installing shingles?
    23.___
    A. 4d   B. 8d   C. 12d   D. 16d

24. A miter joint is cut at a _____° angle.
    24.___
    A. 30   B. 45   C. 60   D. 90

25. Generally, ceiling joists must be braced if the distance between supports is greater than
    25.___
    A. 18 inches   B. 24 inches   C. 4 feet   D. 8 feet

KEY (CORRECT ANSWERS)

1. A		11. B	
2. C		12. A	
3. C		13. C	
4. A		14. D	
5. B		15. B	
6. B		16. B	
7. C		17. B	
8. D		18. B	
9. C		19. C	
10. C		20. A	

21. C
22. C
23. A
24. B
25. D

EXAMINATION SECTION
TEST 1

DIRECTIONS: Each question or incomplete statement is followed by several suggested answers or completions. Select the one that BEST answers the question or completes the statement. *PRINT THE LETTER OF THE CORRECT ANSWER IN THE SPACE AT THE RIGHT.*

Questions 1-2.

DIRECTIONS: Questions 1 and 2 refer to the formula below.

The formula for stopping sight distance SSD13

$$SSD = 1.47tV + \frac{V^2}{30(f+G)}$$

1. The number 1.47 is a(n)   1.___
    A. empirically derived constant
    B. conversion factor
    C. factor based on perception reaction time
    D. factor of safety

2. The term t is usually assumed to be _____ seconds.   2.___
    A. 1.5   B. 2.0   C. 2.5   D. 3.0

3. An automobile weighing W is rounding   3.___
    a curve of radius R with a velocity
    V. Neglecting the friction between
    the tires and the roadway, if the
    forces acting on the car are in
    equilibrium, then

    A. $\sin \theta = \dfrac{V^2}{gR}$

    B. $\cos \theta = \dfrac{V^2}{gR}$

    C. $\tan \theta = \dfrac{V^2}{gR}$

    D. $\cot \theta = \dfrac{V^2}{gR}$

Questions 4-5.

DIRECTIONS: Questions 4 and 5 refer to the horizontal curve below.

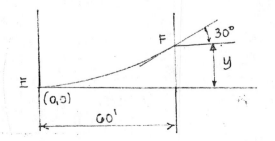

The equation of the curve is $y = kx^3$. The slope of the curve at F is 30°.

4. The value of k is
    A. .000023   B. .000033   C. .000043   D. .000053

    4.___

5. The value of y is
    A. 5.0   B. 7.1   C. 9.3   D. 11.5

    5.___

6. A 4° horizontal curve has a radius of _____ feet.
    A. 1232.4   B. 1332.4   C. 1432.4   D. 1532.4

    6.___

Questions 7-10.

DIRECTIONS: Questions 7 through 10, inclusive, refer to the diagram of a horizontal circular highway curve.

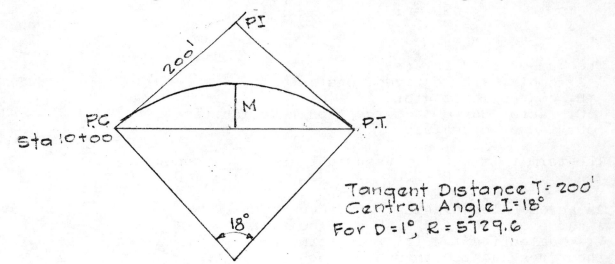

Tangent Distance T = 200'
Central Angle I = 18°
For D = 1°, R = 5729.6

7. The radius of the curve is _____ feet.
    A. 1212.7   B. 1232.7   C. 1262.7   D. 1292.7

    7.___

8. The length of the arc of the circular curve is MOST NEARLY _____ feet.
    A. 396.7   B. 397.0   C. 397.7   D. 398.0

    8.___

9. The long chord P.C. to P.T. is MOST NEARLY _____ feet.
    A. 392.06   B. 393.06   C. 394.06   D. 395.06

    9.___

10. The middle ordinate M is most nearly _____ feet.
     A. 14.95   B. 15.15   C. 15.35   D. 15.55

    10.___

11.   11.___

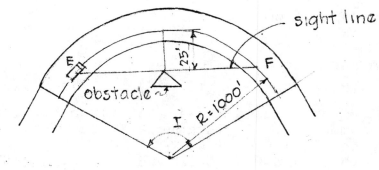

The sight distance EF is MOST NEARLY _____ feet.
   A. 324   B. 364   C. 404   D. 444

12. For crest vertical curves, the length of the curve depends   12.___
     on the change in grade and H_e and H_O where H_e is the
     driver's eye height and H_O is the object height. Their
     relation is usually
         A. $H_e < H_O$
         B. $H_e = H_O$
         C. $H_e > H_O$
         D. H_e is either greater, equal or less than H_O, depend-
            ing on the judgment of chief of design

13. The length of a transition curve which connects a tangent   13.___
     to a circular curve should be sufficient to
         A. keep the rate of change of direction small
         B. achieve the superelevation of the road section
         C. prevent disruption of the drainage system
         D. prevent an abrupt change of direction when the
            circular curve is reached

14. It is desirable to have a minimum road grade of at least   14.___
     0.3% in order to
         A. follow the land contours
         B. facilitate keeping the shoulders clear of debris
         C. secure adequate drainage for the roadway
         D. prevent drivers becoming drowsy on long stretches of
            level roadway

Questions 15-16.

DIRECTIONS: Questions 15 and 16 refer to the horizontal highway
             curve below.

Radius for 1° curve = 5729.6'

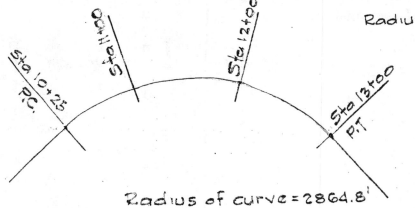

Radius of curve = 2864.8'

15. The deflection angle from the P.C. to Sta 11+00 is   15.___
    A. 0°45'   B. 1°00'   C. 1°15'   D. 1°30'

16. The deflection angle to Sta 13+00 is   16.___
    A. 2°00'   B. 2°45'   C. 3°45'   D. 5°30'

17. Air entrained cement is used in air entrained concrete.   17.___
    The acceptable amount of air is generally between _____
    percent of the total volume.
    A. 1 and 5   B. 2 and 6   C. 3 and 7   D. 4 and 8

18. Pumping of joints in a concrete roadway slab will occur   18.___
    during frequent occurrence of heavy wheel loads, the
    presence in the subgrade soil that is susceptible to
    pumping and
    A. inadequate thickness of the concrete slab
    B. air entrained cement is used in the roadway
    C. surplus water in the subgrade
    D. coarse and fine sand subgrades

19. Distributed steel reinforcing is primarily used to   19.___
    control cracking of a concrete roadway pavement and to
    maintain the integrity of the slab between transverse
    joints. Wire fabric or bar mats are used.
    In a concrete roadway section, the steel is usually placed
    at _____ of the slab.
    A. or near the center
    B. the bottom
    C. the top
    D. the bottom and at the top

20. In slipform paving for a concrete roadway, the slump in   20.___
    the concrete being poured should be _____ inch(es).
    A. ½ to 1   B. 1 to 1½   C. 1½ to 2   D. 2 to 2½

21. The collapse of a section of the New England Thruway at   21.___
    Mianus was due primarily to faulty
    A. steel   B. design
    C. construction   D. periodic inspections

22. The coefficient of expansion of concrete due to tempera-   22.___
    ture change is considered
    A. the same as that for steel
    B. less than that for steel
    C. more than that for steel
    D. more or less than that for steel, depending on the
       type of steel being used

23. Design hourly volume is a future hourly volume used for   23.___
    design. It is usually taken as the _____ hourly volume
    of the year.
    A. 10th   B. 15th   C. 20th   D. 30th

24. Let E be an experiment and S a sample space associated with the experiment. A function X assigned to every element SES a real number X(S) is called a
  A. relative frequency   B. likely outcome
  C. random variable   D. conditional probability

24.___

25. The color code brown on a traffic device denotes
  A. public recreation and scenic guidance
  B. construction and maintenance warning
  C. general warning
  D. motorist service guidance

25.___

———

KEY (CORRECT ANSWERS)

1. B		11. D	
2. C		12. C	
3. C		13. B	
4. D		14. C	
5. D		15. A	
6. C		16. B	
7. C		17. D	
8. A		18. C	
9. D		19. A	
10. D		20. B	

21. D
22. A
23. D
24. C
25. A

TEST 2

DIRECTIONS: Each question or incomplete statement is followed by several suggested answers or completions. Select the one that BEST answers the question or completes the statement. *PRINT THE LETTER OF THE CORRECT ANSWER IN THE SPACE AT THE RIGHT.*

1. The minimum headroom clearance for a sign over a roadway, according to the Federal Highway Administration, should be _____ feet.

   A. 15   B. 16   C. 17   D. 18   1.___

2. In traffic flow, time mean speed _____ space mean speed.   2.___
   A. equals
   B. is less than
   C. is greater than
   D. may be greater or less than

3. Overall speed and running speed are speeds over a   3.___
   relatively long section of street or highway between an
   origin and a destination. Test vehicles are driven over
   the test section of the roadway. The driver attempts to
   float in the traffic stream.
   This means
   A. driving as fast as he can under the speed limit
   B. driving in the middle lane of a three lane road
   C. passing as many vehicles as pass the test vehicle
   D. trying to keep his speed the same as the average
      speed of the vehicles on the road

4. The difference between overall speed and running speed   4.___
   on a test run between origin and destination is overall
   speed is the
   A. average of the maximum and minimum speed while running
      speed is the distance covered divided by the time
      elapsed
   B. distance traveled divided by the time required while
      running speed is the distance traveled divided by
      the time required reduced by time for stop delays
   C. distance traveled divided by the total time required
      while running speed is the minimum time needed to
      cover the distance
   D. distance traveled divided by the total time required
      while running speed is the effort by the driver to
      stay in the flow of traffic

5. The ductility test on asphalt is considered a measure   5.___
   of the _____ of the asphalt.
   A. impact resistance   B. elasticity
   C. durability   D. cementing power

6. In asphalt paving work, there are three different types   6.___
    of specific gravity: bulk, apparent, and effective. Of
    the following statements relating to specific gravity,
    the one that is CORRECT is:
    A. Water absorption is normally not used in determining
       the quantity of permeable voids in the volume of
       aggregates
    B. The apparent specific gravity is less than the bulk
       specific gravity
    C. The effective specific gravity is less than the bulk
       specific gravity
    D. The effective specific gravity falls between the
       bulk specific gravity and the apparent specific
       gravity

7. The temperature range of asphalt prior to entering the   7.___
    mixer in a batch or continuous plant is usually
    A. 150 to 250°F   B. 175 to 275°F
    C. 200 to 300°F   D. 225 to 325°F

8. The most likely cause of the various distress types in   8.___
    asphalt concrete pavements is
    A. structural failure   B. temperature changes
    C. moisture changes   D. faulty construction

9. Bleeding in asphalt concrete pavements is MOST likely   9.___
    caused by
    A. faulty mix composition   B. structural failure
    C. temperature changes   D. moisture changes

10. Depressions in asphalt concrete pavements is MOST likely   10.___
    caused by
    A. faulty construction   B. faulty mix composition
    C. temperature changes   D. moisture changes

11. The gradation curve of particle sizes is represented   11.___
    graphically with the ordinate defining the percent by
    weight passing a given size and the abscissa represent-
    ing the particle size.
    The ordinate is plotted on a(n) _____ scale and the
    abscissa is plotted on a(n) _____ scale.
    A. arithmetic; arithmetic
    B. logarithmic; arithmetic
    C. arithmetic; logarithmic
    D. logarithmic; logarithmic

12. The viscosity of a liquid is a measure of its   12.___
    A. resistance to flow
    B. volatility
    C. solubility in carbon tetrachloride
    D. elasticity

13. Failures that occur in soil masses as a result of the   13.___
    action of highway loads are primarily _____ failures.
    A. tensile   B. torsion   C. shear   D. buckling

14. Bitumens composed primarily of high molecular weight   14.___
    hydrocarbons are soluble in
    A. toluene   B. carbon sulfate
    C. carbon disulfide   D. ammonium chloride

15. One pascal-second equals _____ poise(s).   15.___
    A. 1   B. 5   C. 10   D. 20

16. RS emulsions are best used   16.___
    A. where deep penetration is desired
    B. with coarse aggregates
    C. in warm weather
    D. in spraying applications

17. The specific gravity of bituminous material is generally   17.___
    determined
    A. with a pyenometer   B. with a hygrometer
    C. by displacement   D. with a hydrometer

18. The principal reason for determining the specific gravity   18.___
    of a bituminous material is
    A. converting from volume to weight measurements and
       vice versa
    B. identifying the type of bituminous material used in
       a mix
    C. for checking the uniformity of a mix where large
       quantities are involved
    D. insure that the properties of the mix continue to
       meet specifications

19. The specific gravity of asphaltic products derived from   19.___
    petroleum vary from
    A. .80 to .84   B. .92 to 1.06
    C. 1.04 to 1.18   D. 1.16 to 1.30

20. The flash point is an indirect measurement of the quality   20.___
    and kind of volatiles present in the asphalt being tested.
    Rapid cure cutback asphalts have a flashpoint of _____ or
    less.
    A. 100°F   B. 130°F   C. 150°F   D. 180°F

21. Traffic density is defined as the   21.___
    A. number of vehicles passing a given point in a given
       period of time
    B. average number of vehicles occupying a given length
       of roadway at a given instant
    C. average center to center distance of vehicles on a
       given stretch of roadway at a given instant
    D. minimum distance center to center of vehicles on a
       given stretch of roadway at a given instant

22. Of the following, the best distribution that describes the vehicle distribution on a given stretch of highway at a given instant is the _____ distribution.
    A. Poisson   B. Pascal
    C. normal   D. hypergeometric

22.___

23. In slipform paving for a concrete roadway, the slump in the concrete being poured should be _____ inch(es).
    A. $\frac{1}{2}$ to 1   B. 1 to $1\frac{1}{2}$ C. $1\frac{1}{2}$ to 2   D. 2 to $2\frac{1}{2}$

23.___

24. A water-cement ratio of 6 gallons per sack of cement is equal to a water-cement ratio of _____ by weight.
    A. .50   B. .53   B. .56   C. .59

24.___

25. One micron is equal to _____ centimeters.
    A. 10^{-2} B. 10^{-3} C. 10^{-4} D. 10^{-5}

25.___

KEY (CORRECT ANSWERS)

1. C		11. C	
2. C		12. A	
3. C		13. C	
4. B		14. C	
5. D		15. C	
6. D		16. D	
7. D		17. A	
8. D		18. A	
9. A		19. B	
10. A		20. A	

21. B
22. A
23. B
24. B
25. C

EXAMINATION SECTION
TEST 1

DIRECTIONS: Each question or incomplete statement is followed by several suggested answers or completions. Select the one that BEST answers the question or completes the statement. *PRINT THE LETTER OF THE CORRECT ANSWER IN THE SPACE AT THE RIGHT.*

1. In the future there will be a push for all transportation infrastructure to achieve *sustainable development*. An example of *sustainable development* is
   A. increase the number of lanes on a highway to accommodate added traffic
   B. decrease the number of deaths per million miles of automobile traffic
   C. recycle components of the infrastructure to minimize use of nonrenewable resources
   D. reduce the cost of constructing a mile of highway

   1.___

2. Pressures are mounting to adopt planning and the principles of TQM.
   TQM is the abbreviation for
   A. Transportation Quality Management
   B. Transportation Quality Maintenance
   C. Total Quality Management
   D. Total Quality Maintenance

   2.___

3. Ladybird Johnson's contribution to highways is
   A. the planting of wildflowers adjacent to the highway
   B. the planting of trees along the highways
   C. beautifying highway exits with trees and flowers
   D. improving safety at highway exits

   3.___

4. Bituminous materials used for highways include asphalts and tars derived from destructive distillation of materials such as coal and wood. Tars have been little used recently primarily because of
   A. high cost of the tar
   B. inability to meet the specifications for tar
   C. difficulty in applying this material
   D. lack of availability of the material

   4.___

5. Contraction joints in a Portland cement concrete highway slab are provided in order to
   A. allow the slab to crack at the joint
   B. minimize hydroplaning in wet weather
   C. absorb expansion of the slab
   D. control alligator cracks on the surface of the slab

   5.___

6. Of the following, the one that is designated as a grade of asphalt binder is
   A. AD   B. AS   C. PR   D. PG

   6.___

7. A property of asphaltic materials is viscosity. Viscosity   7.___
   in a liquid is the
   A. resistance to evaporation
   B. tendency to separate into its components
   C. ability of the liquid to mix with other materials
   D. tendency of the liquid to resist flow

8. Medium-curing cutback asphalt contains a _____-type   8.___
   solvent.
   A. kerosene   B. naphtha
   C. heavy fuel oil   D. benzene

9. Asphalt emulsions are becoming the preferred asphalt   9.___
   binder in many agencies because
   A. emulsions are easier to apply
   B. of concern about hydrocarbon emissions from cut-back
      asphalts
   C. emulsions produce an asphalt concrete that is more
      resistant to abrasion
   D. emulsions are more resistant to water penetration

10. An example of vector control on a roadside is   10.___
    A. eliminating a breeding ground for rodent populations
    B. keeping signs and directions in good condition
    C. keeping the roadside free of litter and debris
    D. halting erosion on the roadside

11. An attenuator in highway work is a(n)   11.___
    A. warning device during highway maintenance work
    B. barrier to protect highway maintenance workers
    C. overhead warning to slow down automobiles
    D. crash safety board

12. Preventive maintenance is a planned strategy of cost   12.___
    effective treatment that preserves the system.
    It can BEST be expressed as
    A. don't fix it if it isn't broken
    B. a stitch in time saves nine
    C. if something can go wrong it will
    D. it is preferable to replace than repair

13. There are two types of aggregate used in asphalt mixes: 13.___
    crushed aggregate and round aggregate. Of the following
    statements relating to the two types of aggregate, the
    one that is CORRECT is:
    A. There is no advantage in either aggregate.
    B. Round aggregate is preferable to crushed aggregate.
    C. Crushed aggregate is preferable to round aggregate.
    D. It all depends on the source of the aggregate.

14. Temperature limits should be strictly observed when using   14.___
    asphalt cements. The mixing temperature should be between
    A. 125°F and 175°F   B. 175°F and 225°F
    C. 275°F and 325°F   D. 325°F and 375°F

15. When high early strength is desired in Portland cement concrete, the cement to use is type   15.___
    A. II   B. III   C. IV   D. V

16. The main purpose of grading aggregates in an asphalt roadway mix is to   16.___
    A. provide a good surface
    B. provide a strong mix
    C. minimize the quantity of asphalt required
    D. provide a dense mix to prevent water seepage in the roadway

17. The wearing quality of an aggregate is determined by testing for resistance to   17.___
    A. abrasion   B. crushing
    C. chemical deterioration   D. frost

18. According to the AASHTO Maintenance Manual on Roadways, earth-aggregate roadway surfaces and subsurfaces are most effective when they have achieved at least _____% of their compaction capacity.   18.___
    A. 80   B. 85   C. 90   D. 95

19. Superelevation on a highway usually occurs   19.___
    A. on an approach to a bridge
    B. on a horizontal highway curve
    C. at a high point on a vertical highway curve
    D. at a low point on a vertical highway curve

20. Shoulders have two basic purposes in the roadway system: they provide lanes for emergency or safe travel and they   20.___
    A. prevent vegetation encroaching on the roadway surface
    B. allow seepage into the subgrade of runoff from the roadway surface
    C. provide room for barriers
    D. provide lateral support to the pavement structure

21. For roadway cross-sections without curbs, shoulder cross slopes usually range from _____ for paved surfaces.   21.___
    A. 1% to 3%   B. 3% to 5%   C. 5% to 7%   D. 7% to 9%

22. If turf shoulders are used on a roadway, the advantage of using native grasses usually is that native grasses   22.___
    A. do not need mowing
    B. are more pleasing to the eye than imported grasses
    C. are less expensive than other grasses
    D. do not need irrigation

23. A deep rut in an aggregate shoulder at the edge of a hard-surfaced roadway can usually be corrected by reshaping the shoulder MOST efficiently with a   23.___
    A. scarifier   B. bulldozer
    C. motor grader   D. roller

24. A method of scheduling shoulder maintenance in response   24.__
    to risk management efforts is to
    A. maximize the life of the shoulder
    B. minimize the labor cost of maintaining the shoulder
       in a serviceable condition
    C. defend maintenance policies and practices in the
       event of accident litigation involving the shoulders
    D. use a database to predict when maintenance and repair
       will be required for the shoulders

25. Spalling of the surface of a concrete roadway is   25.__
    generally caused by
    A. inadequate vibrating when pouring the concrete
    B. too low a water/cement ratio in the concrete mix
    C. expansion of the concrete
    D. the use of epoxy-coated reinforcing bars in the
       concrete

———

KEY (CORRECT ANSWERS)

1. C		11. D	
2. C		12. B	
3. A		13. C	
4. D		14. C	
5. A		15. B	
6. D		16. C	
7. D		17. A	
8. A		18. D	
9. B		19. B	
10. A		20. D	

21. B
22. D
23. C
24. C
25. C

———

TEST 2

DIRECTIONS: Each question or incomplete statement is followed by several suggested answers or completions. Select the one that BEST answers the question or completes the statement. *PRINT THE LETTER OF THE CORRECT ANSWER IN THE SPACE AT THE RIGHT.*

1. Corrosion of reinforcing bars in a reinforced concrete road pavement can be caused by water entering the concrete road pavement or _____ entering the concrete road pavement.
   A. sulfates B. chlorides C. carbonates D. fluorides

   1.___

2. A tack coat applied to an old roadway surface creating a bond between the old and the new surface is applied with a distributor at the rate of _____ gallon per square yard.
   A. .05 to .15   B. .15 to .25
   C. .25 to .35   D. .35 to .45

   2.___

3. Some voids should be included in compacted asphaltic concrete to allow for expansion in hot weather. Surface course voids is usually recommended to be
   A. 2% to 4%   B. 4% to 6%   C. 6% to 8%   D. 8% to 10%

   3.___

4. The highest temperature that asphalts can withstand is
   A. 300°F   B. 350°F   C. 400°F   D. 450°F

   4.___

5. A polymer is a substance containing
   A. microscopic air bubbles
   B. the element silicon
   C. a definite lattice arrangement
   D. giant molecules

   5.___

6. The one of the following that is not a polymer concrete is _____ concrete.
   A. epoxy   B. methyl methacrylate
   C. polyurethane   D. vermiculite

   6.___

7. It is suspected that a given stretch of existing roadway may have substructure problems; that is, the soil under the roadway is weak.
   Of the following, the BEST method of testing the sub-surface is with a _____ test.
   A. falling weight deflectometer
   B. soil porosity
   C. consolidation settlement
   D. tiltmeter

   7.___

8. The one of the following that is NOT a claimed potential advantage of using reclaimed asphalt paving for a new asphalt pavement is
   A. energy saving
   B. cost reduction
   C. stronger asphalt pavement
   D. conservation of natural resources

8.__

9. Mineral dust is added to asphalt primarily to _____ asphalt.
   A. make it easier to roll the
   B. increase the viscosity of the
   C. stabilize the
   D. eliminate air pockets in

9.__

10. The smallest size sieve that mineral dust should pass through is No.
    A. 50   B. 100   C. 150   D. 200

10.__

11. Most asphalt used in highway construction is derived from
    A. natural sources   B. coal distillation
    C. inorganic materials   D. petroleum distillation

11.__

12. Asphalt emulsions should be cationic or anionic depending on
    A. the pH value of the asphalt
    B. aggregate size distribution
    C. the pH value of the water used
    D. the type of aggregates used

12.__

13. Air-entrained cement is used in concrete to
    A. expose concrete to severe frost action
    B. give the concrete high early strength
    C. resist sulfate deterioration
    D. make the concrete more workable

13.__

14. The main purpose of vibrating poured concrete is to
    A. eliminate air pockets in the placed concrete
    B. prevent segregation in the concrete
    C. allow excess water to rise to the surface
    D. decrease the water/cement ratio in the poured concrete

14.__

15. The primary purpose of curing a concrete road slab shortly after pouring is primarily to
    A. prevent loss of water in the concrete due to evaporation
    B. protect the concrete from changes in outside temperature
    C. shield the surface of the concrete against the loss of heat
    D. prevent segregation in the concrete slab

15.__

16. A bag of Portland cement weighs MOST NEARLY ____ pounds. 16.___
    A. 82   B. 86   C. 90   D. 94

17. The water/cement ratio for 4,000 pounds per square inch   17.___
    concrete is, in gallons of water per bag of concrete,
    MOST NEARLY
    A. 3   B. 5   C. 7   D. 9

Questions 18-19.

DIRECTIONS: Questions 18 and 19 refer to the notes shown below.

    The notes shown below are used to determine the elevation
    of the top of a manhole M.

Point	BS	HI	F.S.	Elevation
BMA	0.72			151.42'
Manhole M			4.25	

18. The elevation of manhole M is, in feet and inches, MOST   18.___
    NEARLY
    A. 140.45   B. 148.95   C. 153.89   D. 162.39

19. The elevation of manhole M, in feet and inches, is MOST   19.___
    NEARLY
    A. 148'-5 3/8"   B. 148'-11 3/8"
    C. 153'-10 11/16"   D. 162'-4 11/16"

20.   20.___

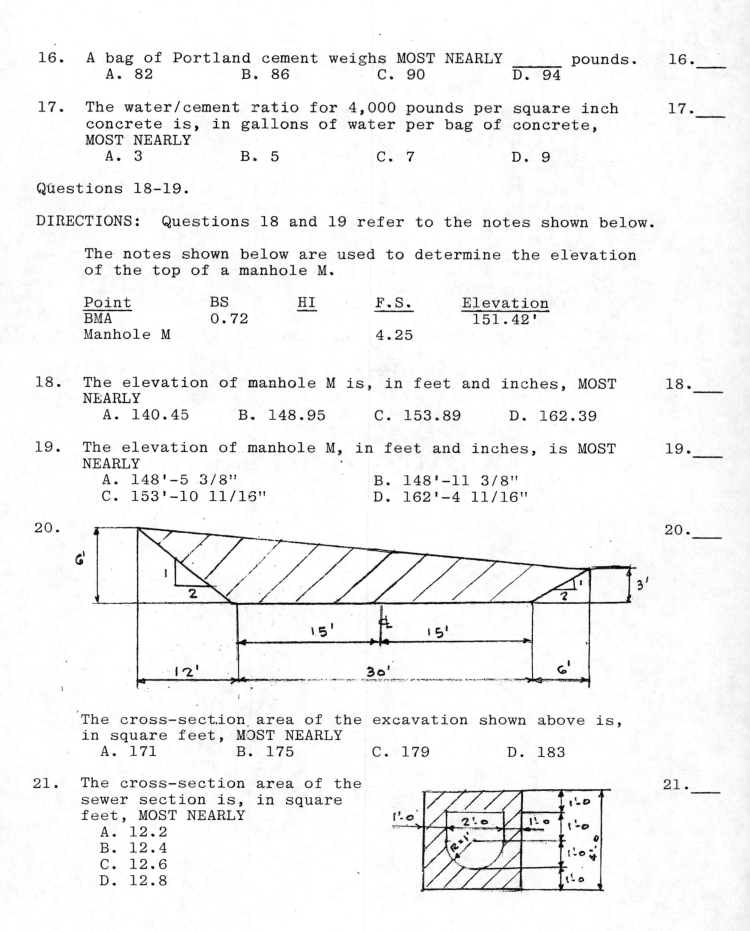

The cross-section area of the excavation shown above is,
in square feet, MOST NEARLY
    A. 171   B. 175   C. 179   D. 183

21. The cross-section area of the   21.___
    sewer section is, in square
    feet, MOST NEARLY
    A. 12.2
    B. 12.4
    C. 12.6
    D. 12.8

22. 3.66 meters is MOST NEARLY _____ feet.
    A. 11   B. 12   C. 13   D. 14

23. In some states litigation has established a legal definition of a safety hazard as any pavement dropoff exceeding
5.1 centimeters. This, in inches, is MOST NEARLY
    A. 1   B. $1\frac{1}{2}$ C. 2   D. $2\frac{1}{2}$

24. In a roadway maintenance manual is a subject heading
titled AESTHETIC OBJECTIVES. An example of an aesthetic
objective is to
    A. reduce highway accidents
    B. enhance a roadway's scenic qualities
    C. improve the roadway's drainage system
    D. widen the roadway at a turnout to prevent vehicles
       backing up into the highway

25. A cubic yard of ordinary unreinforced concrete weighs
MOST NEARLY
    A. 2000   B. 3000   C. 4000   D. 5000

———

KEY (CORRECT ANSWERS)

1. B		11. D	
2. A		12. D	
3. B		13. A	
4. D		14. A	
5. D		15. A	
6. D		16. D	
7. A		17. B	
8. C		18. C	
9. C		19. C	
10. D		20. A	

21. B
22. B
23. C
24. B
25. C

———

EXAMINATION SECTION
TEST 1

DIRECTIONS: Each question or incomplete statement is followed by several suggested answers or completions. Select the one that BEST answers the question or completes the statement. *PRINT THE LETTER OF THE CORRECT ANSWER IN THE SPACE AT THE RIGHT.*

1. In pouring concrete for a large footing, the vibrator is used to move concrete into place.
   This is
   A. *good* practice as it moves the concrete quickly into place
   B. *good* practice as it eliminates air pockets
   C. *poor* practice as it promotes segregation
   D. *poor* practice as it increases pressure against the forms

1.____

2. For successful winter work in placing ordinary concrete, adequate protection against the cold should be provided. Special protection is NOT required when the temperature is over _____ and is required when the temperature is below _____.
   A. 50°F; 50°F
   B. 40°F; 40°F
   C. 30°F; 30°F
   D. 20°F; 20°F

2.____

3. The MAIN reason for curing concrete is to
   A. prevent segregation of the concrete
   B. prevent the formation of air pockets in the concrete
   C. keep the concrete surface moist
   D. minimize bleeding in the poured concrete

3.____

4. Of the following, the concrete mix that uses the greatest amount of cement per cubic yard of concrete is
   A. 1:2:4   B. 1:2:3½   C. 1:2½:5   D. 1:2½:3½

4.____

5. The volume of concrete in a sidewalk 6 ft. x 30 ft. x 4 inches is, in cubic feet, MOST NEARLY
   A. 45   B. 50   C. 55   D. 60

5.____

6. Of the following, the chemical compound that is added to a concrete mix to accelerate setting in cold weather is
   A. potassium chloride   B. calcium chloride
   C. sodium nitrate   D. calcium nitrate

6.____

7. The compressive strength of concrete
   A. reaches a maximum after 28 days
   B. reaches a maximum after 90 days
   C. reaches a maximum after 180 days
   D. increases after 180 days

7.____

8. The smallest size of coarse aggregate for concrete is, 8.___
in inches, MOST NEARLY
   A. 1/4   B. 3/8   C. 1/2   D. 5/8

9. Of the following, the most practical way to determine that 9.___
the water used in a concrete mix is satisfactory is
   A. send a sample to the laboratory
   B. taste the water
   C. the water is also used for drinking
   D. take a sample and let it stand for a while; and if no
      sediment at the bottom of the sample, it is satis-
      factory

10. Grout is 10.___
   A. cement, sand with water added so that it will flow
      readily
   B. cement with water added so that it is fluid
   C. cement and lime with water added so that it will
      flow readily
   D. gravel, sand, and lime with water added so that it
      will flow readily

11. Wire fabric has a designation 4 x 12 6/10. Of the follow- 11.___
ing, the statement that is correct is the _____ center to
center and are _____.
   A. longitudinal wires are 12"; 10 gage
   B. longitudinal wires are 4"; 6 gage
   C. transverse wires are 4"; 6 gage
   D. transverse wires are 12"; 6 gage

12. The volume of a bag of cement is _____ cubic foot(feet). 12.___
   A. 1   B. 1½   C. 2   D. 2½

13. The specifications state: *Forms for slabs shall be set* 13.___
with a camber of ¼ inch for each 10 feet of span. The
purpose of this requirement is to
   A. compensate for deflection
   B. allow for small errors in setting the formwork
   C. allow for shrinkage of the concrete
   D. compensate for settlement of the supports for the
      formwork

14. When an inspector goes out to inspect the reinforcing 14.___
steel before placing of the concrete, the most important
drawings he should have with him are the _____ drawings.
   A. structural steel   B. reinforcing steel detail
   C. formwork   D. erection

15. A reinforcing bar has hooks 15.___
at each end as shown at the
right. The detail drawing
of the bar will show dimension
   A. A
   B. B
   C. C
   D. D

16. Concrete sidewalks are usually finished with a   16.___
    A. screed   B. steel float
    C. wood float   D. darby

17. A new manhole consists of a concrete base made with   17.___
    ordinary cement and a brick superstructure. The minimum
    time that is usually required after the pouring of the
    concrete base to start the brickwork is _____ hours.
    A. 24   B. 48   C. 72   D. 96

18. In a new manhole, the slump in the concrete used in the   18.___
    base should be _____ inches.
    A. 2 to 3   B. 3 to 4   C. 4 to 5   D. 5 to 6

19. The dimensions of a cylinder used for testing the strength   19.___
    of concrete is _____ inch diameter and _____ inches high.
    A. 6; 9   B. 6; 12   C. 8; 9   D. 8; 12

20. The specification for the mixing time required for a   20.___
    concrete mix in a Ready-Mix truck is one minute for a one
    cubic yard batch and a quarter of a minute for every
    additional cubic yard. The minimum mixing time for a ten
    cubic yard batch is _____ minutes.
    A. 2 3/4   B. 3   C. $3\frac{1}{4}$ D. $3\frac{1}{2}$

21. The subgrade for a concrete footing is wetted down before   21.___
    concrete is poured into the footing.
    This is
    A. *poor* practice as the water-cement ratio of the
       concrete will be increased
    B. *poor* practice as it will leave a pocket on the under-
       side of the footing
    C. *good* practice as the water-cement ratio of the con-
       crete will be decreased
    D. *good* practice as the soil will not withdraw water
       from the concrete

22. Concrete should not be poured too rapidly into the form-   22.___
    work for thin walls primarily because
    A. segregation will result
    B. air pockets will form in the wall
    C. there will be excessive pressure on the formwork
    D. there will be seepage of water through the formwork

23. The FIRST step in finishing the surface of a concrete   23.___
    pavement is
    A. darbying   B. floating   C. screeding   D. tamping

24. The grade of a reinforcing steel is 40. The 40 represents   24.___
    the _____ of the steel.
    A. tensile strength   B. ultimate strength
    C. yield point   D. elastic limit

25. In reinforced concrete work, stirrups would MOST likely   25.___
    be found in
       A. beams   B. columns   C. walls   D. footings

—

KEY (CORRECT ANSWERS)

1. C	11. B
2. B	12. A
3. C	13. A
4. B	14. B
5. D	15. D
6. B	16. C
7. D	17. A
8. B	18. A
9. C	19. B
10. A	20. C

21. D
22. C
23. C
24. C
25. A

—

TEST 2

DIRECTIONS: Each question or incomplete statement is followed by several suggested answers or completions. Select the one that BEST answers the question or completes the statement. *PRINT THE LETTER OF THE CORRECT ANSWER IN THE SPACE AT THE RIGHT.*

Questions 1-6.

DIRECTIONS: Questions 1 through 6, inclusive, refer to the following retaining wall.

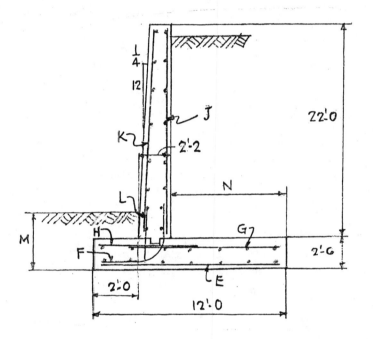

1. The largest size steel bars are most likely to be
   A. H, K, L   B. E, F, J   C. F, G, H   D. F, G, J

1.___

2. Distance M is USUALLY at least
   A. 2'6"   B. 3'0"   C. 3'6"   D. 4'0"

2.___

3. Dimension N is
   A. 7'6   B. 7'8   C. 7'10   D. 8'0

3.___

4. The width of the wall at the top of the wall is
   A. 1'8"   B. 1'8½"   C. 1'9"   D. 1'9½"

4.___

5. The volume of one foot of wall, in cubic feet, is most nearly (neglect the key at the bottom of the wall)
   A. 41.2   B. 41.7   C. 42.2   D. 42.6

5.___

6. The number of cubic yards of concrete in the footing fifty feet long is, in cubic yards, most nearly (neglect the key at the bottom of the wall)
   A. 54.6   B. 55.6   C. 56.6   D. 57.6

6.___

Questions 7-9.

DIRECTIONS: Questions 7 through 9, inclusive, refer to the markings on a reinforcing bar. The end of a reinforcing bar is marked H6N60.

7. The H in H6N60 indicates the 7.___
   A. method of treatment of the reinforcing bar
   B. hardness of the reinforcing steel bar
   C. initial of the steel mill
   D. type of steel in the reinforcing bar

8. The N in the reinforcing steel bar means 8.___
   A. new billet steel
   B. normalized reinforcing steel
   C. the area in which the steel has been produced (north-east)
   D. the initial of the manufacturer

9. The 60 represents the 9.___
   A. ultimate strength of the steel
   B. diameter of the steel in millimeters
   C. allowable unit stress in the steel
   D. grade of the steel

10. The plywood industry produces a special product intended 10.___
    for concrete forming called
    A. structure ply   B. plyform
    C. formply   D. plycoat

11. Lumber that has been inspected and sorted will carry a 11.___
    grade stamp. The item LEAST likely to be found on the
    grade stamp is
    A. state of origin   B. grade
    C. species   D. condition of seasoning

12. In dimensioned lumber, wane indicates 12.___
    A. a lack of lumber
    B. narrow annular rings
    C. undersized width or length of lumber
    D. improper seasoning

13. A sidewalk slab is required to be 4" thick. Measuring 13.___
    down from a nail in the side form that represents the top
    of the slab, the distance is 4½ inches. Of the following,
    the BEST action to take is
    A. have the contractor fill the subgrade with a half
       inch of sand
    B. have the contractor fill the subgrade with a half
       inch of grout
    C. take no action as the contract requirement is met
    D. point out the discrepancy to the contractor and ask
       him to take appropriate action

14. If high visibility is necessary on the job, a vest _____ colored should be worn.   14.___
    A. red   B. orange   C. yellow   D. green

15. Emulsified asphalt tack coats are preferred to using cut-   15.___
back asphalts PRIMARILY because
    A. cut-back asphalts present environmental problems
    B. cut-back asphalts are slower drying than emulsified asphalts
    C. cut-back asphalts are faster drying than emulsified asphalts
    D. emulsified asphalts are easier to place than cut-back asphalts

16. Spread footings are footings that   16.___
    A. cover a large area
    B. have an irregular shape
    C. are sometimes called strap footings
    D. transmit their loads through a combination of piles and soil

17. An excavation for a footing is over-excavated and the   17.___
subgrade is well below the design elevation. Of the
following, the BEST action for the contractor to take is
    A. fill the excavation with well compacted soil until it reaches the design elevation of the bottom of the footing
    B. fill the subgrade with gravel to reach the bottom elevation of the footing
    C. lower the elevation of the footing but retain its thickness
    D. change the footing to a pile supported footing

18. The inspector should be aware of the items in the contract   18.___
that are unit price so that he can
    A. make the proper inspection of these items
    B. keep a record of when they are delivered to the job site
    C. make measurements and compute quantities that may be necessary
    D. record the dates of installation of these items

19. The attitudes that an inspector should adopt in dealing   19.___
with the contractor are to be
    A. understanding and flexible
    B. helpful and cautious
    C. cautious and skeptical
    D. firm and fair

20. Among the provisions for the safety of workers on the job,   20.___
the most basic and general one is
    A. workmen should work slowly
    B. keep alcohol off the job
    C. good housekeeping
    D. wear suitable clothing for extreme weather conditions

21. Ladders should extend a minimum of _____ above the level   21.___
    to which they lead.
    A. six feet   B. knee-high
    C. waist-high   D. five feet

22. An inspector notices a worker working in an unsafe manner.   22.___
    Of the following, the BEST action the inspector can take
    is to
    A. tell the worker the correct way to work
    B. tell the worker's supervisor of the unsafe behavior
       of the worker
    C. record the incident in your log book
    D. notify the contractor so that the unsafe practice
       will cease

23. In making the daily report, personal remarks by the   23.___
    inspector should not be included. Of the following,
    the best reason for this exclusion is
    A. it may raise questions as to the accuracy of the
       report
    B. the wrong people may read the daily report
    C. the inspector should have no opinions
    D. it may indicate bias on the part of the inspector

24. The major difference between a softwood and a hardwood   24.___
    in forestry terms is
    A. the softwoods are from the south and the hardwoods
       are from the north
    B. the softwoods are evergreens and the hardwoods are
       deciduous
    C. the softwoods are soft and the hardwoods are hard
    D. there is one grading method for softwoods and another
       grading method for hardwoods

25. Lumber is considered unseasoned if it has a moisture   25.___
    content of not less than _____ percent in weight of water.
    A. 17   B. 20   C. 23   D. 26

KEY (CORRECT ANSWERS)

1. D	6. B	11. A	16. A	21. C
2. D	7. C	12. A	17. A	22. B
3. C	8. A	13. C	18. C	23. D
4. B	9. D	14. B	19. D	24. B
5. D	10. B	15. A	20. C	25. B

EXAMINATION SECTION
TEST 1

DIRECTIONS: Each question or incomplete statement is followed by several suggested answers or completions. Select the one that BEST answers the question or completes the statement. *PRINT THE LETTER OF THE CORRECT ANSWER IN THE SPACE AT THE RIGHT.*

1. A traffic sign states that parking is permitted on Sundays and Holidays.
   According to the traffic regulations of the city, the holiday on which parking is NOT permitted in the area covered by the sign is
   A. New Year's Day
   B. Memorial Day
   C. Thanksgiving Day
   D. Lincoln's Birthday

   1.___

2. An intrastate bus is a bus that runs
   A. only in one state
   B. in 2 states only
   C. between the United States and Canada
   D. between any states in the Union

   2.___

3. According to the traffic regulations of the Department of Traffic, a pedestrian facing a red signal at an intersection
   A. has the right of way over automobiles having a green signal
   B. has the right of way over trucks having a green signal
   C. may not enter the intersection facing the red signal
   D. may enter the intersection, facing the red signal, if he can do so safely without interfering with traffic

   3.___

4. This sentence was taken from the traffic regulations of the City Department of Traffic with respect to yield signs:
   Proceeding past such sign with resultant collision or other impedance or interference with traffic on the intersecting street shall be deemed prima facie in violation of this regulation.
   The words prima facie mean MOST NEARLY
   A. probably
   B. possibly or likely
   C. literally or completely
   D. guilty

   4.___

5. Where signs on city streets do not indicate otherwise, the MAXIMUM speed limit in the city is, in miles per hour,
   A. 15
   B. 20
   C. 25
   D. 30

   5.___

6. Making a U-turn in the city is NOT permissible on any
   A. street
   B. street in a residential district
   C. street in a business district
   D. 2-way street

   6.___

7. A person stops his car in front of a hydrant and remains
   in the car.
   According to the traffic regulations of the City Department
   of Traffic,
   A. this is illegal if he is within 15 feet of the hydrant
   B. it is legal
   C. he does not have to move if so ordered by a policeman
   D. he may remain there provided he is far enough away
      from the hydrant so as not to interfere with hose
      lines

7.____

8. Taxicabs are
   A. not permitted to cruise
   B. permitted to cruise in residential areas only
   C. permitted to cruise in business areas only
   D. permitted to cruise in all boroughs except Manhattan

8.____

9. Of the following, the one that is the MAIN cause of fatal
   accidents is
   A. direction signals not working
   B. windshield wipers not working
   C. improper alignment of the wheels
   D. defective brakes

9.____

10. The capacity of an approach to an intersection is
    primarily dependent upon
    A. slope of through band   B. cycle length
    C. offsets   D. through band width

10.____

11. To handle heavy traffic movements which tend to cause
    congestion at an intersection, it is often necessary to
    A. use a standard 3-color (RAG) traffic control signal
       on all four corners
    B. add arrow indications to traffic signals permitting
       movements in a certain direction when other traffic
       is halted
    C. use 2-color instead of 3-color traffic signals
    D. install a flasher caution signal facing the direc-
       tion of heavy traffic flow

11.____

12. Elm Street and Oak Street are one-way streets that inter-
    sect.
    A. Cars may turn either right from both streets or left
       from both streets depending on the direction of
       travel.
    B. If cars may turn right into one street, they may not
       turn right into the other.
    C. Only right turns are permitted in both streets.
    D. Only left turns are permitted in both streets.

12.____

13. Of the following intersections where one street dead ends   13.___
into another, the one that is SAFEST is

A.

70°

B.

60°

C.

45°

D.

30°

14. Driver interview, tag on vehicle, and postal cards are   14.___
all methods of obtaining information relative to
   A. vehicle miles traveled
   B. accident data
   C. motor vehicle registration
   D. origin and destination

15. A study of motor vehicle volume normally includes all   15.___
but one of the following:
   A. Directional movements
   B. Motor vehicle occupancy
   C. Motor vehicle classification
   D. Number of vehicles per unit of time

16. Counts made with automatic recorders must always be   16.___
supplemented with manual observations to ascertain
   A. hourly distribution   B. directional distribution
   C. vehicle classification   D. turning movements

17. A cordon count is USUALLY made on a   17.___
   A. weekday   B. Saturday   C. Sunday   D. holiday

18. Of the following vehicles, the one that need NOT be   18.___
stopped at an origin and destination station is a
   A. bus   B. foreign car
   C. station wagon   D. coal truck

19. A turning movement count is USUALLY taken at   19.___
   A. a toll station   B. a highway intersection
   C. a bus terminal   D. the end of a highway

20. A manual traffic count is
    A. a mechanical counter tabulating pedestrians
    B. the number of manuals issued in a traffic survey
    C. an estimated volume of traffic
    D. the number of motor vehicles counted by the person assigned
                                                                    20.___

21. Traffic counts that are made within the city limits are _____ counts.
    A. rural   B. suburban
    C. urban   D. sample
                                                                    21.___

22. When questioning a driver in a traffic survey, the interviewer should
    A. explain briefly the reason for the interview
    B. insist on having his questions answered
    C. get the signature of the person interviewed
    D. report the person interviewed, if he did not cooperate
                                                                    22.___

23. In gathering data for a traffic survey, it was decided to use only the period from 6:00 A.M. to 10:00 P.M. The reason for choosing this period is MOST likely that
    A. employee morale would drop if the inspectors were required to work during the night
    B. the public would not cooperate during the late night or early morning hours
    C. it is inconsiderate to disturb the public in the middle of the night
    D. the information obtained at that time would be considered adequate
                                                                    23.___

24. Of the following data, the one that is MOST significant in a traffic survey is the
    A. locations between which the car travels
    B. number of cars in the driver's family
    C. number of drivers operating the car
    D. average annual mileage of the car
                                                                    24.___

25. The MAIN purpose for making a motor vehicle volume survey of a particular route is to provide basic data for determining
    A. the extent of group riding
    B. whether prevailing speeds are too fast for conditions
    C. a plan of traffic control
    D. where and how much parking space may be needed
                                                                    25.___

26. Of the following studies, the one which is LEAST related and would probably NOT be included in making a traffic safety survey is
    A. street and off-street parking
    B. driver observance of stop signs
    C. pedestrian observance of traffic signals
    D. accident records and facts
                                                                    26.___

27. Of the following, the one which would NOT usually require   27.____
    a traffic survey is
    A. revision of parking time limits to assure most
       efficient usage of curb space
    B. creation of off-street parking facilities
    C. important trends in traffic characteristics and
       transportation demands
    D. complaints from residents in a particular area on
       the disturbance caused by heavy traffic moving
       through that area

28. A *spot-map* is a graphic method which is used to   28.____
    A. show types of traffic signals located at the main
       intersections in a community
    B. analyze the distribution of accidents within a
       community area
    C. arrive at reasonable accident rates
    D. show grades, width, roadway surface, and merging
       traffic streams in a community

29. A survey was made for the purposes of installing traffic   29.____
    control signals at a certain intersection of a main street
    and cross street in a certain area. The survey shows that
    although traffic is relatively heavy during the day, it
    becomes very light at night.
    In such a situation, it would be MOST desirable to
    A. continue the full sequence of indications as in the
       daytime
    B. continue operation of the signals, but lengthen the
       cycle of intervals
    C. completely extinguish the signals leaving the inter-
       section uncontrolled
    D. extinguish the signals but provide a flasher mechanism
       on the controller

30. If the capacity of an approach to an intersection is 3600   30.____
    vehicles per hour of green and the go phase on this
    approach is 40 seconds out of a 60-second cycle, the
    equivalent volume is _____ vehicles per hour.
    A. 2400   B. 3600   C. 5400   D. 2000

31. If a section of a highway 10 miles long carries an annual   31.____
    daily traffic of 5,000 vehicles and there are two deaths
    in a year, the death rate is
    A. 2.0 deaths per 5,000 vehicles
    B. 11.0 deaths per 100 million vehicle miles
    C. 11.0 deaths per million vehicle miles
    D. 2.0 deaths per 50,000 vehicle miles

32. If the difference in elevation between two intersections   32.____
    300 feet apart is 6 feet, the grade along the street is
    A. 2%   B. 2   C. 0.002   D. 6%

33. If on a highway a car passes a given point every 5 seconds,   33.___
    the number of cars per hour passing the given point on the
    highway is
    A. 360   B. 480   C. 600   D. 720

34. The cost of concrete paving for a strip of driveway 50   34.___
    feet long, 10 feet wide, and 6 inches deep, if concrete
    in place costs $30 per cubic yard, is, in dollars, MOST
    NEARLY (27 cubic feet = 1 cubic yard)
    A. 278   B. 318   C. 329   D. 380

Questions 35-38.

DIRECTIONS: Questions 35 through 38 relate to the sketch below.

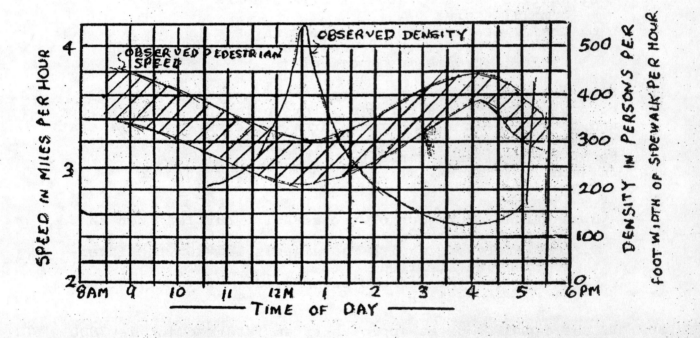

35. Assuming a 10' wide sidewalk, the number of people that   35.___
    would pass the given point at 12:00 M in 10 minutes is
    MOST NEARLY
    A. 580   B. 680   C. 780   D. 880

36. At 10:00 A.M., you could expect a person to be walking   36.___
    at a speed
    A. of 3 miles per hour
    B. between 300 and 420 feet per hour
    C. between 3.2 and 3.65 miles per hour
    D. of 4.5 feet per second

37. The highest average number of people using the sidewalk   37.___
    will USUALLY occur at
    A. 9 A.M.   B. 12:30 P.M.   C. 4 P.M.   D. 5 P.M.

38. Of the following statements relating to the diagram, the   38.___
    one that is MOST NEARLY CORRECT is
    A. the minimum walking speed observed is 2 miles per
       hour
    B. data for the survey was taken continuously for 24
       hours
    C. as the number of people using the sidewalk increases,
       the speed at which they walk decreases
    D. the minimum observed density is 300 people per hour
       per foot width of sidewalk

39. A vehicle moving at 30 miles per hour is moving at a   39.___
    speed, in feet per second, MOST NEARLY
    A. 30   B. 44   C. 52   D. 60

40. A street map is to a scale 1 inch equals 600 feet. A   40.___
    distance of ½ inch on the drawing represents a distance
    on the ground, in feet, MOST NEARLY
    A. 300   B. 600   C. 900   D. 1,200

Questions 41-42.

DIRECTIONS: Questions 41 and 42 refer to the sketches below.

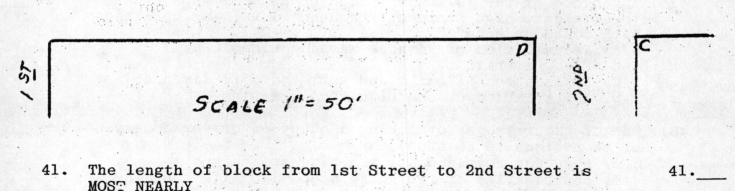

41. The length of block from 1st Street to 2nd Street is   41.___
    MOST NEARLY
    A. 150'   B. 250'   C. 350'   D. 450'

42. The northeast corner of Main and 2nd is   42.___
    A. A   B. B   C. C   D. D

43. The sketch shown at the right
    shows a right triangular island
    at the intersection of three
    streets on which is installed
    traffic signals A and B.
    Traffic conditions have
    increased and require than an
    additional traffic light be
    installed at point C. Electric
    power for signal C is to be
    taken from the junction box
    located at the base of post A
    and extended to C as shown by
    the broken line.
    With the distances given as shown, the length of conduit,
    in feet, required to extend power from A to C is MOST
    NEARLY

    A. 44   B. 60   C. 83   D. 75

43.____

44. The volume of traffic at a certain location increased
    from 1,000 to 1,500 vehicles per hour.
    The percentage increase of traffic is MOST NEARLY

    A. 33%   B. 50%   C. 60%   D. 40%

44.____

45. A collision diagram would MOST likely NOT show

    A. direction of movement of each vehicle or pedestrian
       involved
    B. distance of the accident to the nearest building line
    C. date and hour of the accident
    D. weather and road conditions

45.____

46. A graphical representation of the detailed nature of
    accidents occurring at a location is known as a

    A. collision diagram   B. condition diagram
    C. accident summary   D. accident spot map

46.____

47. Which one of the following remedies is MOST appropriate
    to eliminate high accident frequency involving collisions
    with fixed objects?

    A. Installation of advance warning signs
    B. Reroute traffic
    C. Application of paint and reflectors to fixed object
    D. Installation of center dividing strip

47.____

48. One of the reasons for making a study of driver observance
    of stop signs is to study the

    A. need for retaining or removing stop signs
    B. desirability of replacing stop sign with a police
       officer
    C. desirability of installing pedestrian crosswalk lines
    D. need for speed zoning

48.____

49. Which one of the following remedies is MOST appropriate   49.___
    to eliminate high accident frequency involving pedestrian-
    vehicular collisions at intersections?
    A. Installation of turning guide lines
    B. Installation of painted pavement lane lines
    C. Installation of pedestrian cross-walk lines
    D. Removal of view obstruction

50. The driver of a vehicle approaching a yield sign is   50.___
    required to
    A. proceed without changing speed
    B. slow down if there is a vehicle in the intersection
    C. stop
    D. slow down and proceed with caution

———

KEY (CORRECT ANSWERS)

1. D	11. B	21. C	31. B	41. B
2. A	12. B	22. A	32. A	42. C
3. C	13. A	23. D	33. D	43. B
4. C	14. D	24. A	34. A	44. B
5. C	15. B	25. C	35. A	45. B
6. C	16. C	26. A	36. C	46. A
7. A	17. A	27. D	37. B	47. C
8. A	18. A	28. B	38. C	48. A
9. D	19. B	29. D	39. B	49. C
10. D	20. D	30. A	40. A	50. D

TEST 2

1. No person shall stop, stand, or park a vehicle closer to a fire hydrant than
   A. 17'   B. 10'   C. 15'   D. 12'   1.____

2. When stopping is prohibited by signs or regulations and no conflict exists with other traffic, the driver of a vehicle is
   A. permitted to stop temporarily
   B. not permitted to stop
   C. permitted to stand
   D. permitted to park   2.____

3. Where there is a *No Parking* sign, a person may
   A. not stop his vehicle
   B. stop his vehicle to discharge passengers
   C. stop his vehicle and leave it unattended for a maximum of 10 minutes
   D. stop his vehicle and leave it unattended for a maximum of 5 minutes   3.____

4. Of the following, the MOST restrictive parking sign is
   A. no standing   B. no parking
   C. taxi stand   D. bus stop   4.____

5. A highway sign that is classified as a <u>Guide</u> sign is
   A. Stop   B. No Passing
   C. Narrow Road   D. North Bound   5.____

6. A highway sign that is classified as a <u>Warning</u> sign is
   A. No U Turn   B. Hill
   C. Speed Limit 50   D. Do Not Enter   6.____

7. A highway sign that is classified as a <u>Regulatory</u> sign is
   A. One Way   B. Men Working
   C. RR   D. Detour   7.____

8. A traffic device that has the same effect as a stop sign is a
   A. flashing yellow   B. flashing red
   C. yield sign   D. detour sign   8.____

9. A warrant for a certain type of traffic control device is a(n)
   A. official order to install the device
   B. application from a local community for the device
   C. reason for installing the device
   D. request to remove the device   9.____

10. Shapes of signs on state highways convey
    definite information.
    The sign to the right means
    A. steep hill - slow down
    B. come to a full stop
    C. you may proceed with caution
    D. approaching narrow bridge

10.____

11. Where flasher mechanisms must be installed at intersec-
    tions of a main street and a cross street as a warning
    signal, it would be BEST to have flashing
    A. amber on the main street and flashing red on the
       cross street
    B. red on the main street and flashing amber on the
       cross street
    C. red on the main street only
    D. amber on the cross street only

11.____

12. The primary purpose of *progressive timing* of traffic
    control signals is to
    A. allow the largest volume of traffic flow at the
       safest speed along a particular route
    B. permit slow drivers to travel at an increased speed
    C. permit the largest volume of pedestrian traffic to
       cross safely at the same time
    D. reduce traveling speed so that motorists have vehicles
       under constant control

12.____

13. A hazard marker, for example, at the end of a dead-end
    street, would MOST likely be
    A. yellow background with black letters
    B. yellow background with red letters
    C. a reflector type marker
    D. a warning sign

13.____

14. Of the following, the BEST reason for having markings
    that are uniform in design, position, and application
    is that
    A. less skill is required to provide the markings
    B. they cost less when they are uniform
    C. there is no harm done in providing them even where
       there is no need
    D. they may be recognized and understood instantly

14.____

15. If numerous pedestrian accidents occur at a signalized
    intersection, a pertinent study to help evaluate the
    problem would be
    A. signal timing
    B. motor vehicle volume
    C. pedestrian observance of traffic signals
    D. driver observance of pedestrian right of way

15.____

16. Which one of the following types of fixed-time signal   16.___
    systems is MOST desirable?
    _____ system.
        A. Flexible progressive   B. Alternate
        C. Simple progressive   D. Simultaneous

17. Of the following statements relating to traffic actuated   17.___
    signals, the one that is CORRECT is
        A. it is especially useful at little used intersections
        B. the length of time the green light is on is not
           constant
        C. it can only be used at the intersection of one-way
           streets
        D. it can only be used at the intersection of two-way
           streets

18. An advantage of the three lens signal (red, yellow, and   18.___
    green) over the two lens signal (red and green) is that it
        A. enables cars within the intersection to clear
        B. allows pedestrians to cross the intersection safely
        C. may be operated as a traffic actuated signal
        D. may be used as a caution signal when not used as a
           stop and go signal

19. A fixed time signal is one by which traffic stops and goes 19.___
        A. for equal time periods
        B. according to a predetermined time schedule
        C. by manual control
        D. according to the volume of traffic

20. The proper installation of vehicle detectors is MOST   20.___
    important for a
        A. pedestrian push-button installation
        B. fixed time signal system
        C. traffic actuated signal
        D. progressive system

21. Of the following, the one that is NOT considered a dis-   21.___
    advantage in the use of pavement markings is they
        A. may be obliterated by snow
        B. may not be clearly visible when wet
        C. must be used with other devices such as traffic signs
           or signals
        D. are subject to traffic wear

22. *It is often desirable to mark lines on the pavement to*   22.___
    indicate the limits and the clearance of the overhang
    on turning streetcars.
    This safety measure is NOT required in this city because
        A. there are no streetcars in this city
        B. city traffic is controlled by other suitable devices
        C. city traffic is not fast enough to require it
        D. streetcars in this city turn only at the depot and
           not in the streets

23. A yellow curb marking may be used at all but one of the following:
    A. A fire hydrant
    B. A bus stop
    C. A depressed curb leading to a loading platform
    D. Where parking is prohibited from 8 A.M. to 6 P.M.

23.___

24. Stop lines or limit lines are used to indicate
    A. parking space limits to prevent encroachment on a fire hydrant zone
    B. the marking of stalls where parking meters are used
    C. the point behind which vehicles must stop in compliance with a traffic signal
    D. where pedestrians are permitted to cross a street

24.___

25. An island, as applied to traffic control,
    A. provides a safe area for a traffic patrolman
    B. segregates pedestrians and vehicles
    C. provides a clear area for a bus stop
    D. establishes a barrier between opposite lanes of traffic

25.___

26. Of the following, the one which is NOT a method for providing channelization of traffic is by
    A. permanent islands or strips
    B. pavement markings
    C. use of stanchions
    D. mounting traffic signal at center of intersection

26.___

27. The PRIMARY purpose for marking the pavement of heavily traveled thoroughfares into lanes is to
    A. slow up traffic
    B. prevent accidents
    C. speed up traffic
    D. keep slow drivers on the right side of the road

27.___

28. When parking is not otherwise restricted in the city, no person shall park a commercial vehicle in excess of _____ hours.
    A. 2   B. 4   C. 3   D. 6

28.___

29. A condition which need NOT be considered in making a general parking survey is
    A. reasons for parking at various locations
    B. street and roadway widths and surfaces
    C. average time vehicles remained at various locations
    D. sidewalk obstructions, such as lamp posts and fire posts

29.___

30. Concerning the purpose of parking meters, the statement which is NOT true is
    A. assist in reducing overtime parking at the curb
    B. increase parking turnover
    C. eliminate the need for off-street parking facilities
    D. facilitate enforcement of parking regulations

30.___

31. The MOST efficient layout of parking spaces in a large lot   31.___
is to place the stalls _____ to the aisles.
    A. parallel   B. at right angles
    C. at a 30° angle   D. at a 60° angle

32. The time limits set by cities for parking on city streets   32.___
during the daytime
    A. is considered strictly a policing problem
    B. is shorter in concentrated business areas
    C. will vary directly with the amount of traffic on the
       street
    D. is uniform for all sections of the city

33. Four parts of a survey report are listed below, not   33.___
necessarily in their proper order:
    I. Body of report   II. Synopsis of report
    III. Letter of transmittal   IV. Conclusions
Which one of the following represents the BEST sequence
for inclusion of these parts in a report?
    A. III, IV, I, II   B. II, I, III, IV
    C. III, II, I, IV   D. I, III, IV, II

34. A traffic control inspector recommends that an illuminated   34.___
advertising sign near a signal light be removed.
The reason for this recommendation is MOST likely that
    A. a driver's attention may be attracted to the sign
       rather than the road
    B. the similarity of colors may cause confusion
    C. such signs mar the beauty of the roadside
    D. the sign encroaches upon public property

35. Of the following, the MOST important value of a good   35.___
report is that it
    A. reflects credit upon the person who submitted the
       report
    B. provides good reference material
    C. expedites official business
    D. expresses the need for official action

36. The MOST important requirement in report writing is   36.___
    A. promptness in turning in reports
    B. length
    C. grammatical construction
    D. accuracy

37. You have discovered an error in your report submitted to   37.___
the main office.
You should
    A. wait until the error is discovered in the main office
       and then correct it
    B. go directly to the supervisor in the main office after
       working hours and ask him unofficially to correct the
       answer

C. notify the main office immediately so that the error can be corrected if necessary
D. do nothing, since it is possible that one error will have little effect on the total report

38. The use of *radar* by police as a means of apprehending motorists who exceed the speed limit has recently been challenged in court on the grounds that
    A. the motorists are not forewarned
    B. the speed limits have not been posted
    C. the equipment does not give reliable results
    D. there is no sworn evidence that a speed violation took place

    38.____

39. Of the following, the one which is generally classified as a commercial vehicle is a
    A. station wagon
    B. chauffeur-driven passenger car
    C. taxicab
    D. truck

    39.____

40. A divided arterial highway for through traffic with full or partial control of access is generally referred to as an
    A. expressway   B. parkway
    C. freeway   D. major street

    40.____

41. Of the following, the MOST important advantage to be gained by converting a two-way north-south street to a one-way street is
    A. *decrease* the number of accidents
    B. *decrease* the need for bus service
    C. *increase* the average speed of traffic
    D. *increase* the turnover at curbs

    41.____

42. Of the following, the BEST road for heavy traffic is
    A. two lane   B. three lane
    C. four lane undivided D. four lane divided

    42.____

43. When weekend traffic differs greatly from weekday traffic,
    A. the average daily traffic figure is used in estimating weekend traffic
    B. weekend traffic counts should be made as well as weekday counts
    C. the traffic count for another road in the area should be used
    D. traffic counts should be made at different seasons of the year

    43.____

44. Work is now going on to approximately double the car-carrying capacity of which one of the following?
    A. Car parkways   B. Bridges
    C. Tunnels   D. HOV lanes

    44.____

45. The MOST recent major change in the specifications of   45.____
the federally aided highway program is
   A. increasing the permissible grades or roads
   B. requirements for drainage
   C. lane width
   D. vertical clearance under bridges

46. A recent newspaper article reported that small cars are   46.____
considered a danger to the federally aided highway
program.
Of the following, the one that may be considered as the
reason for this danger is
   A. they consume less gas providing less taxes for the
      highway program
   B. the lanes of the new highways are too wide for these
      cars, disorganizing the traffic flow pattern
   C. the two-car family is upsetting the estimates of
      traffic flow
   D. foreign cars are hurting American business

47. Span-wire mountings of fixed traffic control signals is   47.____
generally
   A. used in the city at heavily traveled intersections
   B. used in the city at intersections in isolated areas
   C. not used in the city
   D. used at locations where more than two streets inter-
      sect

48. A map depicting straight lines drawn from points of   48.____
vehicle origin to points of vehicle destination is
known as a _____ map.
   A. desire line   B. traffic flow
   C. bar   D. pie

49. Brake reaction time for most people is APPROXIMATELY   49.____
_____ seconds.
   A. 0.6   B. 2.0   C. 0.1   D. 1.4

50. Trucks should travel along prescribed truck routes if   50.____
their overall length is equal to or exceeds
   A. 27'   B. 41'   C. 30'   D. 33'

KEY (CORRECT ANSWERS)

1. C	11. A	21. C	31. B	41. C
2. B	12. A	22. A	32. B	42. D
3. B	13. C	23. D	33. C	43. B
4. A	14. D	24. C	34. B	44. D
5. D	15. C	25. B	35. C	45. D
6. B	16. A	26. D	36. D	46. A
7. A	17. B	27. C	37. C	47. C
8. B	18. D	28. C	38. C	48. A
9. C	19. B	29. D	39. D	49. A
10. B	20. C	30. C	40. A	50. D

EXAMINATION SECTION

TEST 1

DIRECTIONS: Each question or incomplete statement is followed by several suggested answers or completions. Select the one that Best answers the question or completes the statement. *PRINT THE LETTER OF THE CORRECT ANSWER IN THE SPACE AT THE RIGHT.*

Questions 1-4.

DIRECTIONS: Answer Questions 1 to 4 based on the information given in the traffic volume table below.

TRAFFIC VOLUME COUNTS

Time (A.M.)	Main Street Northbound	Southbound	Cross Street Eastbound	Westbound
7:00- 7:15	100	100	70	60
7:15- 7:30	110	100	80	70
7:30- 7:45	150	140	110	100
7:45- 8:00	170	160	140	130
8:00- 8:15	210	190	120	110
8:15- 8:30	180	170	90	80
8:30- 8:45	160	140	70	60
8:45- 9:00	150	160	70	50
9:00- 9:15	140	150	50	50
9:15- 9:30	130	120	40	20
9:30- 9:45	120	110	30	30
9:45-10:00	120	100	30	30

1. The hour during which traffic, moving in both directions on Main Street, reached its *peak* was
   A. 7:30 - 8:30   B. 7:45 - 8:45
   C. 8:00 - 9:00   D. 8:15 - 9:15

1.___

2. The hour during which traffic volume, moving in both directions on Cross Street, reached its *peak* was
   A. 7:30 - 8:30   B. 7:45 - 8:45
   C. 8:00 - 9:00   D. 8:15 - 9:15

2.___

3. The HIGHEST average hourly volume over the three-hour period 7:00 to 10:00 was recorded for
   A. Main Street northbound   B. Main Street southbound
   C. Cross Street eastbound   D. Cross Street westbound

3.___

4. The *peak* 15-minute traffic volume for all directions of travel occurred between
   A. 7:30 - 7:45   B. 7:45 - 8:00
   C. 8:00 - 8:15   D. 8:15 - 8:30

4.___

5. Which of the following statements relating to one-way streets is CORRECT?
   One-way streets
   A. increase turning movement conflicts between vehicles
   B. decrease street capacity
   C. decrease accident hazards for pedestrians
   D. make it impossible to time traffic signals to control speeds

5.___

Questions 6-11.

DIRECTIONS: Answer Questions 6 to 11 based on the information given in Figure I below.

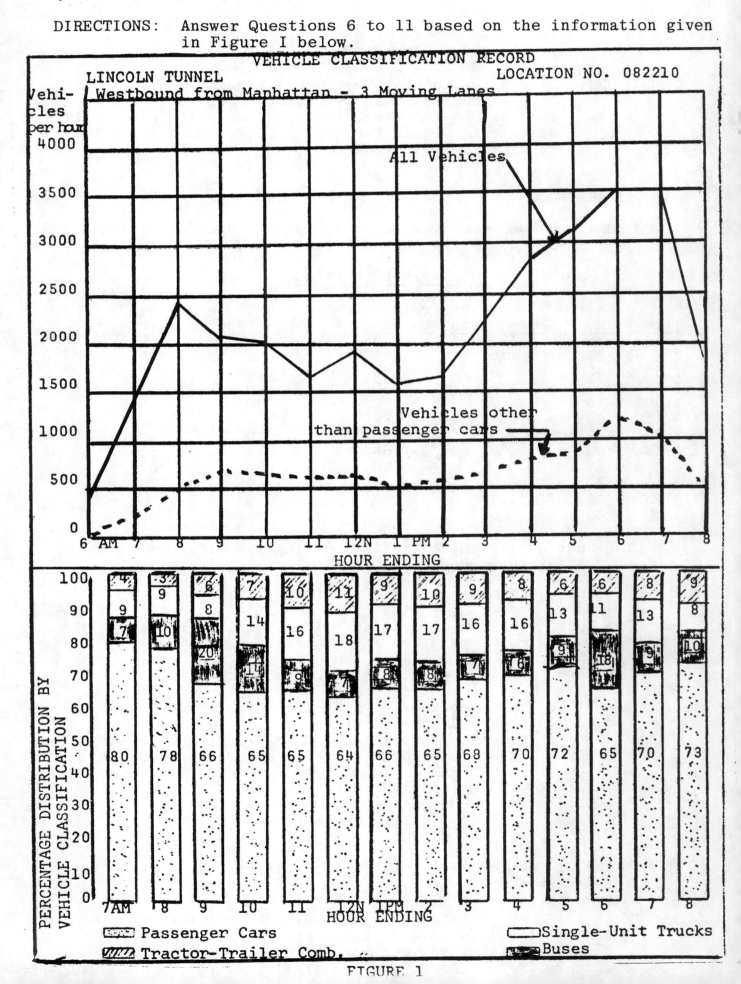

FIGURE 1

6. The total number of all vehicles traveling through the Lincoln Tunnel westbound from Manhattan between the hours of 6 A.M. and 12 Noon is *most nearly*
    A. 5,500   B. 7,500   C. 9,500   D. 11,500

    6.___

7. The number of passenger cars recorded during the hour ending at 7 P.M. was *most nearly*
    A. 235   B. 1160   C. 2450   D. 3500

    7.___

8. Excluding passenger cars, the AVERAGE number of vehicles per moving lane recorded during the peak hour was *most nearly*
    A. 420   B. 1180   C. 1250   D. 3550

    8.___

9. The percentage of buses recorded between 6 A.M. and 8 P.M. ranged between
    A. 3% and 11%   B. 8% and 18%
    C. 6% and 20%   D. 64% and 80%

    9.___

10. During the study period, the percentage of single unit trucks *exceeded* the percentage of buses for ____ hours.
    A. 4   B. 5   -C. 9   D. 10

    10.___

11. For all vehicles recorded, the recorded traffic volume during the morning peak hour was *most nearly* ____ of the volume during the evening peak hour.
    A. 40%   B. 50%   C. 60%   D. 70%

    11.___

12. In urban areas, traffic volume is usually LOWEST during the month of
    A. January   B. March   C. August   D. October

    12.___

13. In urban shopping areas, the *peak* traffic activity USUALLY occurs during
    A. Monday afternoon and Friday night
    B. Friday night and Saturday afternoon
    C. Thursday night and Saturday afternoon
    D. Monday night and Friday night

    13.___

14. In the metric system, the unit that is closest to a mile is a
    A. centimeter   B. liter
    C. millimeter   D. kilometer

    14.___

Questions 15-16.

DIRECTIONS: Questions 15 and 16 refer to the diagram at the top of the following Page 4.

15. Vehicle X in the diagram is heading in which direction?
    A. Southeast   B. Southwest
    C. Northeast   D. Northwest

    15.___

16. If Vehicle X in the diagram makes a right turn at the intersection, it will be headed
    A. southeast   B. southwest
    C. northeast   D. northwest

    16.___

17. The one of the following that is NOT a function of
channelization is
A. control the angle of conflict
B. favor certain turning movements
C. protect pedestrians
D. increase the pavement area within an intersection

17.___

18. The time of display of the yellow signal indication
following the green signal indication is called the
A. clearance interval   B. time cycle
C. traffic phase   D. interval sequence

18.___

19. A lane constructed for the purpose of allowing vehicles
entering a highway to increase speed to a rate that is safe
for merging with through traffic is called a(n) _____ lane.
A. auxiliary   B. through
C. acceleration   D. deceleration

19.___

20. A traffic volume count which records the number and types
of vehicles passing a given point is called a _____ count.
A. rate-of-flow   B. capacity
C. classification   D. roadway

20.___

21. On highways, the MAIN purpose served by barriers between
traffic going in opposite directions is to
A. stop cars if they get out of lane
B. minimize the glare from oncoming cars
C. prevent cars from overturning if they have blowouts
D. prevent head-on accidents

21.___

22. Control count stations are USUALLY used to
A. establish seasonal and daily traffic volume
characteristics
B. make short manual traffic counts
C. classify traffic
D. count traffic on weekends only

22.___

23. The MAIN purpose of off-center traffic lanes is to
    A. protect slow-moving traffic from the hazards of fast-moving traffic
    B. permit the use of special traffic control
    C. provide additional capacity in one direction of travel
    D. provide a slow-down area for disabled vehicles

23.____

24. Reserved transit lanes are used to
    A. make sure buses stop at the curb
    B. reduce bus and passenger car accidents
    C. decrease transit travel times by reducing friction between buses and other vehicles
    D. make it easier for people to get on and off buses

24.____

25. The slope or grade between points X and Y shown in the diagram below is
    A. 4%   B. 10%   C. 25%   D. 50%

25.____

KEY (CORRECT ANSWERS)

1. B		11. D	
2. A		12. A	
3. A		13. B	
4. C		14. D	
5. C		15. B	
6. D		16. D	
7. C		17. D	
8. A		18. A	
9. C		19. C	
10. C		20. C	

21. D
22. A
23. C
24. C
25. A

TEST 2

DIRECTIONS: Each question or incomplete statement is followed by several suggested answers or completions. Select the one that BEST answers the question or completes the statement. *PRINT THE LETTER OF THE CORRECT ANSWER IN THE SPACE AT THE RIGHT.*

1. In the city, when parking is not otherwise restricted, commercial vehicles can park
   A. up to a maximum of one hour
   B. up to a maximum of three hours
   C. up to a maximum of eight hours
   D. without a time limitation

   1.___

2. In the city, with respect to loading an parking, commercial vehicles are allowed to
   A. load or unload merchandise expeditiously in a no-standing zone
   B. park for one hour in a no-parking zone
   C. load or unload merchandise expeditiously in a no-parking zone
   D. park for one hour in a no-standing zone

   2.___

3. On the Federal national highway system, highways ending in an even number run
   A. in the east-west direction
   B. both east-west or north-south
   C. in the north-south direction
   D. around cities and not through them

   3.___

4. The *current* maximum allowed speed limit on Federal interstate highways is ____ miles per hour.
   A. 50   B. 55   C. 60   D. 65

   4.___

5. In the city, when a vehicle is too long for a single parking meter space, the vehicle may
   A. not be parked in the parking meter area
   B. be parked using more than one space but a coin must be deposited in the meter designated for each space occupied
   C. be parked using more than one space and a coin must be deposited only in the forward parking meter
   D. be parked using more than one space and a coin must be deposited only in the rear parking meter

   5.___

6. In the city, some signs indicate that stopping, standing, or parking regulations are in effect every day except Sundays. Where this sign is used, stopping, standing, or parking regulations would apply on
   A. Washington's Birthday   B. Brooklyn Day
   C. Columbus Day   D. Election Day

   6.___

7. In the city, unless signs are posted indicating specific   7.___
   hours during which play street regulations are in effect,
   such regulations are in effect on designated streets FROM
   A. 7 A.M. until 4 P.M.
   B. 8 A.M. until ½ hour before sunset
   C. 8 A.M. to ½ hour after sunset
   D. 8 A.M. to 8 P.M.

8. When preparing to make a turn while driving a vehicle on   8.___
   a roadway, a driver should signal his intention to turn
   AT LEAST ____ feet in advance of the turn.
   A. 50   B. 100   C. 150   D. 200

9. Unless otherwise permitted or prohibited by posted signs,   9.___
   the MAXIMUM continuous period during which a vehicle may
   be parked on any roadway in the city is ____ hours.
   A. 8   B. 12   C. 24   D. 48

10. In the city, commercial vehicles may angle stand or angle   10.___
    park in
    A. any area where no parking signs are installed, provided
       the street is wide enough to allow the vehicle to
       park at an angle
    B. on any one-way street where standing is not prohibited,
       provided the street is wide enough to allow the
       vehicle to park at an angle
    C. on a two-way street in areas authorized by signs,
       provided that the vehicle shall not occupy more than
       a parking lane plus one moving lane
    D. on a two-way street in areas authorized by signs,
       provided that the vehicles shall not extend more
       than 10 feet from the curb

11. Which of the following is MOST restrictive to drivers of   11.___
    passenger cars?
    A. Regulations relating to parking in front of fire
       hydrants
    B. No parking regulations
    C. No standing regulations
    D. No stopping regulations

12. The MAXIMUM permitted speed limit in the city, unless   12.___
    signs indicate otherwise, is ____ mph.
    A. 25   B. 30   C. 35   D. 40

13. With regard to right-of-way at an intersection that is   13.___
    NOT controlled by a traffic control device, the one of
    the following statements that is CORRECT is
    A. the car on your right has the right-of-way
    B. the car on your left has the right-of-way
    C. a car preparing to enter the intersection has the
       right-of-way over a car in the intersection
    D. a car turning left has the right-of-way over a
       vehicle going straight ahead

14. At an intersection controlled by traffic signals, a red   14.___
    arrow pointing to the right means that a right turn may
       A. be made after coming to a full stop
       B. be made providing the driver yields the right-of-way
          to all other vehicles and pedestrians
       C. not be made during the period that the red arrow is
          illuminated
       D. be made only if there is another indication showing
          a round green signal light

15. A flashing red traffic signal has the SAME meaning as a   15.___
       A. stop sign
       B. yield sign
       C. flashing yellow traffic signal
       D. hazardous intersection warning sign

16. Traffic signals are MOST frequently installed to reduce   16.___
    ____ collision accidents.
       A. right-angle   B. rear-end
       C. side-swipe   D. head-on

17. The CORRECT color combination for warning signs is   17.___
       A. yellow lettering or symbols on a black background
       B. white lettering or symbols on a red background
       C. black lettering or symbols on a yellow background
       D. black lettering or symbols on a white background

18. A PROGRESSIVELY timed traffic signal system will   18.___
       A. turn all the signals red or green at the same time
       B. usually increase the number of rear-end accidents
          but reduce the number of right-angle accidents
       C. make it more hazardous for pedestrians to cross at
          the signalized intersections
       D. decrease the number of stops traffic is required to make

19. The EFFECT of traffic signals on accidents is that   19.___
    traffic signals
       A. always decrease accidents
       B. sometimes increase accidents
       C. never increase accidents
       D. have no real effect on accidents

20. With respect to traffic devices, which of the following   20.___
    situations should receive the LOWEST priority in terms
    of repair or replacement?
       A. Inoperative or malfunctioning traffic signals at an
          intersection
       B. Missing "No Standing - Rush Hour" regulation signs
       C. Missing "Yield" signs controlling the intersection
          of a minor street with a major street
       D. Inoperative parking meters along one block in a
          retail shopping area

21. Of the following, the BEST reason why a stop sign would be 21.___
    used instead of a yield sign to control traffic at an
    intersection is
       A. there are a larger number of rear-end accidents on
          the street being controlled

B. the street being controlled is less than 36 feet wide
C. visibility is limited at the intersection
D. the approaches to the intersection are offset to each other

22. The USUAL color combination used on interstate signs is ___ lettering and symbols on a ___ background.　22.___
    A. white; green　　　　　　B. green; white
    C. white; black　　　　　　D. black; white

23. The geometrical shape of a railroad crossing sign is that of a(n)　23.___
    A. octagon　　B. circle　　C. rectangle　　D. triangle

24. The STANDARD pedestrian walking speed used in timing pedestrian signals is ___ per second.　24.___
    A. 1 foot　　B. 4 feet　　C. 8 feet　　D. 12 feet

25. A driver approaching an intersection where a sign authorizes a right turn on a red traffic signal indication may make such a turn AND　25.___
    A. has the right-of-way over all vehicles in the intersection
    B. must yield right-of-way to all vehicles and pedestrians within the intersection
    C. must yield right-of-way only to vehicles and pedestrians on the cross street
    D. has the right-of-way over other turning vehicles

KEY (CORRECT ANSWERS)

1. B		11. D	
2. C		12. B	
3. A		13. A	
4. B		14. C	
5. C		15. A	
6. B		16. A	
7. C		17. C	
8. B		18. D	
9. C		19. B	
10. C		20. D	

21. C
22. A
23. B
24. B
25. B

EXAMINATION SECTION
TEST 1

DIRECTIONS: Each question or incomplete statement is followed by
several suggested answers or completions. Select the
one that BEST answers the question or completes the
statement. *PRINT THE LETTER OF THE CORRECT ANSWER IN
THE SPACE AT THE RIGHT.*

1. When making a preliminary inspection of a new street
   marking job, the FIRST thing to check is whether
      A. the location is correct
      B. all dimensions are correct
      C. the right paint is specified
      D. traffic can easily be controlled

1.____

2. After a preliminary inspection of a new street marking job
   has been made and it has been found that it can be laid
   out exactly as shown in the drawings received from Plans
   and Surveys, the site should be reinspected on the first
   day of actual work to check that
      A. the dimensions are correct according to the plans
      B. the orientation has not changed
      C. excavation work that did not exist on his first
         inspection does not obstruct his work
      D. the traffic can easily be controlled

2.____

3. Of the following, it is MOST important when inspecting
   the installation of a sign in a garage or on a street to
   check for the _____ the sign.
      A. correct width of
      B. correct area of
      C. correct mounting height of
      D. removal of all scuff marks below

3.____

4. When inspecting a job site in an off-street parking
   garage prior to starting a new job involving markings,
   the FIRST thing to look for is
      A. obstructions such as beams which will require that
         the layout be altered
      B. oil on the floor
      C. paint splashes on the floor
      D. vehicles which must be moved

4.____

5. The one of the following items which should be checked on
   a job involving the installation of custom-made highway
   guide signs but which need NOT be checked during the
   installation of street regulatory signs is the _____ of
   the sign.
      A. color   B. wording and spelling
      C. width   D. area

5.____

6. Assume that you are facing east while standing on the
    ·northwest corner of the intersection of two streets. One
    of these streets runs north and south, and the other runs
    east and west.
    The SOUTHWEST corner of this intersection is
    A. *directly* across the street in front of you
    B. *directly* across the street to your right
    C. *diagonally* across the intersection from you
    D. *directly* across the street to your left

6.___

7. A street running north and south intersects a street
    running east and west. Four men designated as A, B, C,
    and D are each on a different corner of the intersection.
    A is on the NW corner and faces east; B is on the SW
    corner and faces north; C is on the SE corner and faces
    west; and D is on the NE corner and faces west.
    The two men who are facing DIRECTLY toward each other are
    A. A and B   B. B and C   C. C and D   D. A and D

7.___

8. Of the following, the MOST important item to check during
    a routine inspection of an air compressor is the
    A. amount of air used daily
    B. number of hours it has been operated
    C. diaphragm diameter
    D. condition of the paint finish

8.___

9. Assume that a crew assigned to you goes out to paint some
    street markings on a street which has a great deal of
    traffic.
    The traffic should be diverted away from the working
    area by means of
    A. Class I barricades
    B. Class II barricades
    C. Class I barricades and cones
    D. cones

9.___

10. Assume that an extensive area within an off-street park-
    ing facility has caved in.
    Until repairs are completed, cars should be kept away
    from this area by means of
    A. Class I barricades
    B. Class I barricades and flasher lights
    C. Class II barricades and cones
    D. warning signs and Class I barricades

10.___

11. A line of traffic cones, being used to divert traffic
    from men painting cross-walks in the lane nearest the
    curb, should begin at the curb at a point whose distance
    from the working area is _____ feet, and the cones
    should be _____ feet apart.
    A. 40; 10   B. 60; 15   C. 80; 15   D. 100; 10

11.___

12. Crews doing street marking work at night should wear   12.___
    A. gray coveralls and set out traffic cones to divert
       traffic away from the area
    B. reflectorized vests and set out traffic cones to
       divert traffic away from the area
    C. bright yellow helmets and gray coveralls
    D. bright blue helmets and set out traffic cones to
       divert traffic away from the area

13. Assume that the top of a 12 foot ladder is to be placed   13.___
against a wall.
The RECOMMENDED safe practice is that the ladder should
be placed so that the distance from the bottom of the
ladder to the base of the wall is _____ ft.
    A. 1   B. 2   C. 3   D. 5

14. According to the State Vehicle and Traffic Law, when   14.___
driving at a speed of 40 miles per hour along a dry road,
the driver should maintain a distance between his car
and the car immediately ahead of him of AT LEAST _____
car lengths.
    A. 2   B. 3   C. 4   D. 5

15. Assume that a man has been knocked unconscious.   15.___
Which of the following should NOT be done to the victim?
    A. Give him something to drink
    B. Hold a handkerchief with spirits of ammonia under
       his nose if he is breathing
    C. Keep him covered with a blanket
    D. Give him artificial respiration if he is not breath-
       ing

16. A paint sprayer may have gauges showing the pressure of   16.___
the tank, the paint pressure, and the atomizer pressure.
When the sprayer is operating properly, the
    A. paint pressure is higher than the tank pressure
    B. atomizer pressure is higher than the tank pressure
    C. paint and atomizer pressures are equal
    D. atomizer pressure is higher than the paint pressure

17. A certain paint can cover 310 square feet per gallon.   17.___
The number of gallons of this paint required to paint
200 lines each 6 inches wide and 18 feet-6 inches long
is MOST NEARLY
    A. 2   B. 4   C. 6   D. 8

18. Paint brushes that are used with an oil-based paint are   18.___
USUALLY cleaned with
    A. turpentine   B. linseed oil
    C. acetone   D. alcohol

19. The air in an air compressor cylinder is DIRECTLY com-   19.___
pressed by the
    A. pressure switch   B. surge chamber
    C. cam   D. piston

20. The part which permits the motor of an air compressor to   20.___
    start free of load regardless of the tank pressure is
    the
    A. unloader valve   B. surge tank
    C. pressure switch   D. drain cock

21. Assume that instead of spraying paint properly, a paint   21.___
    sprayer ejects a solid stream of paint from its nozzle.
    The one of the following that may cause this condition is
    A. compressor tank pressure is too high
    B. compressor tank pressure is lower than the atomizer
       pressure
    C. atomizer pressure is higher than the paint pressure
    D. atomizer pressure is too low

22. The one of the following which is a *regulatory* sign is the   22.___
    A. bump sign   B. low clearance sign
    C. route marker   D. stop sign

23. The one of the following which is a *regulatory* sign is   23.___
    the _____ sign.
    A. yield   B. stop ahead
    C. side road   D. slippery when wet

24. The one of the following signs which is octagonal is the   24.___
    _____ sign.
    A. speed limit   B. stop ahead
    C. road narrows   D. stop

25. Of the following statements, the one which gives the   25.___
    function of a *warning* sign is that this sign
    A. indicates route designations, destinations, or dis-
       tances
    B. gives the driver notice of laws or regulations that
       apply at a given place, disregard of which is
       punishable as a violation or a misdemeanor
    C. calls attention to conditions in or adjacent to a
       street that are potentially hazardous to traffic
    D. indicates points of interest or geographical loca-
       tions

26. The regulation manual on temporary traffic control of the   26.___
    department of traffic defines Class II barricades as
    being of the *horse* type with only one rail.
    It further specifies that the rail should be marked on
    A. *one* side with 3" vertical red and white, black and
       white, or black and yellow reflectorized stripes
    B. *both* sides with 3" vertical red and white, black and
       white, or black and yellow stripes
    C. *both* sides with 6" reflectorized red and white, black
       and white, or black and yellow stripes sloping at an
       angle of 45°
    D. *both* sides with 6" vertical red and white or black
       and white stripes

27. Silk screening is a method of 27.___
    A. temporarily concealing signs already erected but
       not ready to be used
    B. painting signs
    C. protecting newly painted crosswalks until they dry
    D. protecting reflectorized signs from dust

28. The blade of a snow plow is USUALLY made of 28.___
    A. monel   B. steel
    C. tungsten carbide   D. beryllium

29. To PROPERLY check the lifting device of a snow plow at 29.___
   the beginning of the snow season, the plow blade should
   be
    A. raised and kept in that position for at least three
       minutes in order to detect leaks in the system
    B. raised by the lifting device once to see if it
       operates
    C. dropped quickly after being brought to the raised
       position
    D. raised and lowered and then the operation should be
       repeated

30. At the present time, the department of traffic USUALLY 30.___
   reflectorizes signs by
    A. coating the portion of the sign to be reflectorized
       with very tiny glass beads held by an adhesive base
    B. outlining the reflectorized portion of the sign with
       large glass *bull's eyes*
    C. making the reflectorized portion of the sign with
       Scotch Lite
    D. painting the reflectorized portion of the sign with
       Luminar

KEY (CORRECT ANSWERS)

1. A	11. D	21. D
2. C	12. B	22. D
3. C	13. C	23. A
4. A	14. C	24. D
5. B	15. A	25. C
6. B	16. D	26. C
7. D	17. C	27. B
8. B	18. A	28. B
9. D	19. D	29. A
10. C	20. A	30. C

EXAMINATION SECTION
TEST 1

DIRECTIONS: Each question or incomplete statement is followed by several suggested answers or completions. Select the one that BEST answers the question or completes the statement. *PRINT THE LETTER OF THE CORRECT ANSWER IN THE SPACE AT THE RIGHT.*

1. Your car's brakes transform one type of energy into another.
   Which of the following BEST describes the change?
   A. Kinetic energy into heat
   B. Centrifugal force into force of impact
   C. Gravity into kinetic energy
   D. Centrifugal force into heat

   1.___

2. Which of the following qualities is MOST important in driving a motor vehicle?
   A. Fast reaction time   B. Courage
   C. Skill   D. Judgment

   2.___

3. Glaring headlights add to night driving hazards.
   Which of the following should you NOT do?
   A. Lower your headlight beams in advance of meeting other cars
   B. Reduce your speed when facing headlight glare
   C. Focus your eyes downward on the center line of the road instead of up into the oncoming lights
   D. Lower your headlight beams when following another car

   3.___

4. The following institutions lend money for the purchase of cars.
   Which charges the LOWEST rate of interest?
   A. Banks
   B. Pawnshops
   C. Installment finance companies
   D. Personal loan companies

   4.___

5. Under what conditions do we find the GREATEST traction?
   A. Wet concrete pavement
   B. Dry concrete pavement
   C. Dry concrete pavement with sand on it
   D. Bumpy, uneven pavement

   5.___

6. Your danger zone is
   A. the longest distance at which you can see and recognize danger
   B. your stopping distance
   C. the distance at which a vehicle in back of your car is following
   D. your braking distance

   6.___

7. For sound financing of a purchase of an automobile, you   7.___
   would have to raise a down payment of AT LEAST _____ of
   the value of the car.
      A. 10 percent   B. 25 percent
      C. one-third   D. one-half

8. Which of the following is characteristic of older paved   8.___
   roads and not of modern highways?
      A. Median strips   B. High road crowns
      C. Road banking   D. Long sight distances

9. Designed especially for slowing down to prepare to leave   9.___
   the freeway is the
      A. deceleration lane   B. median strip
      C. ramp   D. road shoulder

10. When you find yourself getting very sleepy while driving   10.___
    on a long trip, the BEST remedy is
       A. black coffee   B. fresh air
       C. Benzedrine   D. sleep

11. Which of these four types of insurance does a bank or   11.___
    other lender require the purchaser to have?
       A. Collision   B. Comprehensive
       C. Liability   D. Medical payment

12. The professional specialist who plans the operation of   12.___
    highways is the
       A. Commissioner of Motor Vehicles
       B. highway engineer
       C. traffic engineer
       D. Commissioner of State Police

13. Which of the following is the CORRECT formula?   13.___
       A. Braking distance + stopping distance = reaction
          distance
       B. Reaction distance + stopping distance = braking
          distance
       C. Reaction distance + braking distance = stopping
          distance
       D. Reaction distance + danger zone = stopping distance

14. Which of the following is a YIELD sign?   14.___

       A.   B.   C.   D.

15. When you drive around a curve, which of the following   15.___
    helps you to do it safely?
       A. Centrifugal force   B. Friction
       C. Kinetic energy   D. Force of impact

16. If you are involved in an accident, which of the follow-   16.___
ing things should you NOT do?
   A. Show your driver's license and vehicle registration
      card and make note of the information on those of
      the driver of the other car.
   B. If any person seems to be seriously injured, place
      him in your car immediately and proceed at once to
      the nearest hospital.
   C. Submit accident reports as indicated by your state
      and local regulations.
   D. Notify your insurance company.

17. No person should drive in dense fog unless it is absolute- 17.___
ly necessary.
   When it does prove necessary, he should use
   A. parking lights
   B. high-beam headlights
   C. low-beam headlights
   D. no lights, to avoid distortion of vision

18. Under which of the following would you classify the   18.___
wearing of glasses to aid vision?
   A. Compensation   B. Field of vision
   C. Correction   D. Adjustment

19. The key words for driving on a slippery surface are 19.___
   A. firmly and accurately B. gently and gradually
   C. strongly and steadily   D. quickly and surely

20. Which of the following types of insurance is MOST impor- 20.___
tant to a car owner?
   A. Collision   B. Liability
   C. Comprehensive   D. Medical payment

KEY (CORRECT ANSWERS)

1. C		11. A	
2. D		12. C	
3. D		13. C	
4. A		14. D	
5. B		15. A	
6. B		16. B	
7. C		17. C	
8. B		18. C	
9. A		19. B	
10. D		20. B	

TEST 2

1. Which of these four items is a *grade separation*?   1.___
   A. A divided highway
   B. A change in the slope of a hill
   C. Bushes planted between two roadways on which traffic moves in opposite directions
   D. A cloverleaf

2. Which of the following blood alcohol concentrations should   2.___
   be used to establish that a driver is *under the influence of alcohol*?
   A. 0.05%   B. 0.10%   C. 0.15%   D. 0.6%

3. Three of the following four statements are true of free-   3.___
   ways. Which statement is NOT true?
   A. They have a limited number of interchanges at which vehicles may enter or leave the freeway.
   B. They have a limited number of STOP and GO signals.
   C. Traffic moving in opposite directions is not separated by a median strip.
   D. Crossing the median strip is not permitted.

4. To correct a skid, you should   4.___
   A. steer in the direction in which the rear of the car is skidding
   B. steer in the direction opposite that in which the rear of the car is skidding
   C. hold the steering wheel firmly in the straight-ahead position
   D. use the parking or handbrake so that only the rear wheels will lock while the front wheels turn freely

5. The MOST dangerous effects of alcohol on the driver are   5.___
   those concerned with
   A. vision
   B. reaction time
   C. behavior
   D. coordination and driving skill

6. The *Three E's* of traffic safety are included in the   6.___
   following four words.
   Which of them is NOT one of the *Three E's*?
   A. Education   B. Engineering
   C. Enforcement   D. Efficiency

7. Which of the following BEST describes the true meaning
   of the word *courage*?
   A. Ability to overcome fear
   B. Absence of fear
   C. Taking chances to gain a reputation as a daredevil
   D. Lack of realization of the true nature of danger

   7.___

8. Which of the following types of insurance is of GREATEST
   importance to you when you own a car?
   A. Liability   B. Collision
   C. Comprehensive   D. Medical payment

   8.___

9. Which of the following statements is NOT correct?
   A. Most states have legalized the use of electric
      directional signals to signal turns.
   B. Overheating is always due to failures in the cooling
      system.
   C. Power brakes do not decrease the stopping distance.
   D. The horn should never be sounded except in the
      interest of safety.

   9.___

10. Three of the following are good safety features.
    Which is NOT a safety feature?
    A. Door locks
    B. Rear-view mirror inside the car
    C. Eye-level outside mirror
    D. Ventilation of the inside of the car

    10.___

11. The MOST important factor in good car maintenance is
    A. an honest, dependable service station or garage
    B. a skilled mechanic
    C. high quality, reliable parts
    D. a responsible car owner

    11.___

12. Three of the following procedures will add to tire trac-
    tion in starting your car on ice.
    Which one will NOT help?
    A. Letting some air out of the rear tires
    B. Sprinkling sand on the ice
    C. Slipping the clutch
    D. Feeding gas more gently and more gradually

    12.___

13. The four-stroke cycle includes THREE of the following.
    Which of the following is NOT part of the cycle?
    _____ stroke.
    A. Intake   B. Compression
    C. Power   D. Completion

    13.___

14. Vehicles A, C, and D in the illus-   14.___
    tration shown at the right have
    stopped to allow vehicle B to
    turn.
    Which vehicle, A, C, or D, would
    be the FIRST to cross the inter-
    section, considering right-of-
    way rules?
    A. A
    B. C
    C. D
    D. None of the above

15. What part of the cost of planning, designing, and con-   15.___
    structing the National System of Interstate and Defense
    Highways is paid for by Federal-aid funds?
    A. 90%   B. 50%   C. 10%   D. 100%

16. When you leave a freeway and drive on a city street, you   16.___
    must check your speed frequently because you may be
    A. accelerated
    B. suffering from highway hypnosis
    C. velocitized
    D. suffering impairment of vision due to carbon
       monoxide

17. Which of the following statements is CORRECT?   17.___
    A. Certain drugs, like Benzedrine in *keep-awake* pills,
       actually make driving at night safe.
    B. A driver should trust no one but a physician to
       determine whether or not he should drive after
       taking any kind of drug.
    C. The Federal Food and Drug Act does not permit the
       sale of any drug dangerous to a driver without a
       prescription from a registered physician.
    D. The individual driver must rely entirely upon his
       judgment and knowledge of how a specific drug will
       affect him.

18. Three of the following four maintenance procedures are   18.___
    good.
    Which is NOT a good procedure?
    A. Rotate your tires to avoid uneven wear.
    B. Avoid letting oil or gasoline come into contact with
       your tires.
    C. For driving in very hot weather, underinflate your
       tires to avoid building up excessive pressure in
       them.
    D. Keep the battery terminals covered with a light layer
       of grease.

19. Drivers should be able to recognize traffic signs by   19.____
    their shape.
    Which of the following signs warns drivers that they
    are approaching a railroad grade crossing?
    A.   B.   C.   D.

20. Imagine that the steering wheel is the face of a clock.   20.____
    The driver's hands should grasp it at _____ and _____
    o'clock.
    A. 8; 4   B. 9; 3   C. 10; 2   D. 11; 1

KEY (CORRECT ANSWERS)

1. D	11. C
2. A	12. A
3. B	13. D
4. A	14. C
5. D	15. A
6. C	16. C
7. A	17. B
8. A	18. C
9. B	19. B
10. C	20. C

EXAMINATION SECTION
TEST 1

DIRECTIONS: Each question or incomplete statement is followed by several suggested answers or completions. Select the one that BEST answers the question or completes the statement. *PRINT THE LETTER OF THE CORRECT ANSWER IN THE SPACE AT THE RIGHT.*

1. Which of the following is the MOST likely action a supervisor should take to help establish an effective working relationship with his departmental superiors?   1.____

    A. Delay the implementation of new procedures received from superiors in order to evaluate their appropriateness.
    B. Skip the chain of command whenever he feels that it is to his advantage.
    C. Keep supervisors informed of problems in his area and the steps taken to correct them.
    D. Don't take up superiors' time by discussing anticipated problems but wait until the difficulties occur.

2. Of the following, the action a supervisor could take which would *generally* be MOST conducive to the establishment of an effective working relationship with employees includes   2.____

    A. maintaining impersonal relationships to prevent development of biased actions
    B. treating all employees equally without adjusting for individual differences
    C. continuous observation of employees on the job with insistence on constant improvement
    D. careful planning and scheduling of work for your employees

3. Which of the following procedures is the LEAST likely to establish effective working relationships between employees and supervisors?   3.____

    A. Encouraging *two-way* communication with employees
    B. Periodic discussion with employees regarding their job performance
    C. Ignoring employees' gripes concerning job difficulties
    D. Avoiding personal prejudices in dealing with employees

4. Criticism can be used as a tool to point out the weak areas of a subordinate's work performance.
Of the following, the BEST action for a supervisor to take so that his criticism will be accepted is to   4.____

    A. focus his criticism on the act instead of on the person
    B. exaggerate the errors in order to motivate the employee to do better
    C. pass judgment quickly and privately without investigating the circumstances of the error
    D. generalize the criticism and not specifically point out the errors in performance

5. In trying to improve the motivation of his subordinates, a supervisor can achieve the BEST results by taking action based upon the assumption that most employees   5.____

    A. have an inherent dislike of work
    B. wish to be closely directed
    C. are more interested in security than in assuming responsibility
    D. will exercise self-direction without coercion

6. When there are conflicts or tensions between top management and lower-level employ-   6.___
ees in any department, the supervisor should FIRST attempt to

    A. represent and enforce the management point of view
    B. act as the representative of the workers to get their ideas across to management
    C. serve as a two-way spokesman, trying to interpret each side to the other
    D. remain neutral, but keep informed of changes in the situation

7. A probationary period for new employees is usually provided in many agencies.   7.___
The MAJOR purpose of such a period is *usually* to

    A. allow a determination of employee's suitability for the position
    B. obtain evidence as to employee's ability to perform in a higher position
    C. conform to requirements that ethnic hiring goals be met for all positions
    D. train the new employee in the duties of the position

8. An effective program of orientation for new employees usually includes all of the follow-   8.___
ing EXCEPT

    A. having the supervisor introduce the new employee to his job, outlining his respon-
       sibilities and how to carry them out
    B. permitting the new worker to tour the facility or department so he can observe all
       parts of it in action
    C. scheduling meetings for new employees, at which the job requirements are
       explained to them and they are given personnel manuals
    D. testing the new worker on his skills and sending him to a centralized in-service
       workshop

9. In-service training is an important responsibility of many supervisors.   9.___
The MAJOR reason for such training is to

    A. avoid future grievance procedures because employees might say they were not
       prepared to carry out their jobs
    B. maximize the effectiveness of the department by helping each employee perform
       at his full potential
    C. satisfy inspection teams from central headquarters of the department
    D. help prevent disagreements with members of the community

10. There are many forms of useful in-service training. Of the following, the training method   10.___
which is NOT an appropriate technique for leadership development is to

    A. provide special workshops or clinics in activity skills
    B. conduct institutes to familiarize new workers with the program of the department
       and with their roles
    C. schedule team meetings for problem-solving, including both supervisors and lead-
       ers
    D. have the leader rate himself on an evaluation form periodically

11. Of the following techniques of evaluating work training programs, the one that is BEST is to

    A. pass out a carefully designed questionnaire to the trainees at the completion of the program
    B. test the knowledge that trainees have both at the beginning of training and at its completion
    C. interview the trainees at the completion of the program
    D. evaluate performance before and after training for both a control group and an experimental group

11._____

12. Assume that a new supervisor is having difficulty making his instructions to subordinates clearly understood.
The one of the following which is the FIRST step he should take in dealing with this problem is to

    A. set up a training workshop in communication skills
    B. determine the extent and nature of the communications gap
    C. repeat both verbal and written instructions several times
    D. simplify his written and spoken vocabulary

12._____

13. A director has not properly carried out the orders of his assistant supervisor on several occasions to the point where he has been successively warned, reprimanded, and severely reprimanded.
When the director once again does not carry out orders, the PROPER action for the assistant supervisor to take is to

    A. bring the director up on charges of failing to perform his duties properly
    B. have a serious discussion with the director, explaining the need for the orders and the necessity for carrying them out
    C. recommend that the director be transferred to another district
    D. severely reprimand the director again, making clear that no further deviation will be countenanced

13._____

14. A supervisor with several subordinates becomes aware that two of these subordinates are neither friendly nor congenial.
In making assignments, it would be BEST for the supervisor to

    A. disregard the situation
    B. disregard the situation in making a choice of assignment but emphasize the need for teamwork
    C. investigate the situation to find out who is at fault and give that individual the less desirable assignments until such time as he corrects his attitude
    D. place the unfriendly subordinates in positions where they have as little contact with one another as possible

14._____

15. A DESIRABLE characteristic of a good supervisor is that he should

    A. identify himself with his subordinates rather than with higher management
    B. inform subordinates of forthcoming changes in policies and programs only when they directly affect the subordinates' activities
    C. make advancement of the subordinates contingent on personal loyalty to the supervisor
    D. make promises to subordinates only when sure of the ability to keep them

15._____

16. The supervisor who is MOST likely to be successful is the one who   16.____

    A. refrains from exercising the special privileges of his position
    B. maintains a formal attitude toward his subordinates
    C. maintains an informal attitude toward his subordinates
    D. represents the desires of his subordinates to his superiors

17. Application of sound principles of human relations by a supervisor may be expected to   17.____
    _____ the need for formal discipline.

    A. decrease   B. have no effect on
    C. increase   D. obviate

18. The MOST important generally approved way to maintain or develop high morale in   18.____
one's subordinates is to

    A. give warnings and reprimands in a jocular manner
    B. excuse from staff conferences those employees who are busy
    C. keep them informed of new developments and policies of higher management
    D. refrain from criticizing their faults directly

19. In training subordinates, an IMPORTANT principle for the supervisor to recognize is that   19.____

    A. a particular method of instruction will be of substantially equal value for all employees in a given title
    B. it is difficult to train people over 50 years of age because they have little capacity for learning
    C. persons undergoing the same course of training will learn at different rates of speed
    D. training can seldom achieve its purpose unless individual instruction is the chief method used

20. Over an extended period of time, a subordinate is MOST likely to become and remain   20.____
most productive is the supervisor

    A. accords praise to the subordinate whenever his work is satisfactory, withholding criticism except in the case of very inferior work
    B. avoids both praise and criticism except for outstandingly good or bad work performed by the subordinate
    C. informs the subordinate of his shortcomings, as viewed by management, while according praise only when highly deserved
    D. keeps the subordinate informed of the degree of satisfaction with which his performance of the job is viewed by management

KEY (CORRECT ANSWERS)

1.	C	11.	D
2.	D	12.	B
3.	C	13.	A
4.	A	14.	D
5.	D	15.	D
6.	C	16.	D
7.	A	17.	A
8.	D	18.	C
9.	B	19.	C
10.	D	20.	D

TEST 2

1. A supervisor has just been told by a subordinate, Mr. Jones, that another employee, Mr. Smith, deliberately disobeyed an important rule of the department by taking home some confidential departmental material.
   Of the following courses of action, it would be MOST advisable for the supervisor first to

   A. discuss the matter privately with both Mr. Jones and Mr. Smith at the same time
   B. call a meeting of the entire staff and discuss the matter generally without mentioning any employee by name
   C. arrange to supervise Mr. Smith's activities more closely
   D. discuss the matter privately with Mr. Smith

1.____

2. The one of the following actions which would be MOST efficient and economical for a supervisor to take to minimize the effect of periodic fluctuations in the work load of his unit is to

   A. increase his permanent staff until it is large enough to handle the work of the busy loads
   B. request the purchase of time and labor saving equipment to be used primarily during the busy loads
   C. lower, temporarily, the standards for quality of work performance during peak loads
   D. schedule for the slow periods work that is not essential to perform during the busy periods

2.____

3. Discipline of employees is usually a. supervisor's responsibility. There may be several useful forms of disciplinary action.
   Of the following, the form that is LEAST appropriate is the

   A. written reprimand or warning
   B. involuntary transfer to another work setting
   C. demotion or suspension
   D. assignment of added hours of work each week

3.____

4. Of the following, the MOST effective means of dealing with employee disciplinary problems is to

   A. give personality tests to individuals to identify their psychological problems
   B. distribute and discuss a policy manual containing exact rules governing employee behavior
   C. establish a single, clear penalty to be imposed for all wrongdoing irrespective of degree
   D. have supervisors get to know employees well through social mingling

4.____

5. A recently developed technique for appraising work performance is to have the supervisor record on a continual basis all significant incidents in each subordinate's behavior that indicate unsuccessful action and those that indicate poor behavior.
Of the following, a MAJOR disadvantage of this method of performance appraisal is that it

    A. often leads to overly close supervision
    B. results in competition among those subordinates being evaluated
    C. tends to result in superficial judgments
    D. lacks objectivity for evaluating performance

5.____

6. Assume that you are a supervisor and have observed the performance of an employee during a period of time. You have concluded that his performance needs improvement.
In order to improve his performance, it would, therefore, be BEST for you to

    A. note your findings in the employee's personnel folder so that his behavior is a matter of record
    B. report the findings to the personnel officer so he can take prompt action
    C. schedule a problem-solving conference with the employee
    D. recommend his transfer to simpler duties

6.____

7. When an employee's absences or latenesses seem to be nearing excessiveness, the supervisor should speak with him to find out what the problem is.
Of the following, if such a discussion produces no reasonable explanation, the discussion usually BEST serves to

    A. affirm clearly the supervisor's adherence to proper policy
    B. alert other employees that such behavior is unacceptable
    C. demonstrate that the supervisor truly represents higher management
    D. notify the employee that his behavior is being observed and evaluated

7.____

8. Assume that an employee willfully and recklessly violates an important agency regulation. The nature of the violation is of such magnitude that it demands immediate action, but the facts of the case are not entirely clear. Further, assume that the supervisor is free to make any of the following recommendations.
The MOST appropriate action for the supervisor to take is to recommend that the employee be

    A. discharged   B. suspended
    C. forced to resign   D. transferred

8.____

9. Although employees' titles may be identical, each position in that title may be considerably different.
Of the following, a supervisor should carefully assign each employee to a specific position based PRIMARILY on the employee's

    A. capability   B. experience
    C. education   D. seniority

9.____

10. The one of the following situations where it is MOST appropriate to transfer an employee to a similar assignment is one in which the employee

    A. lacks motivation and interest
    B. experiences a personality conflict with his supervisor

10.____

C. is negligent in the performance of his duties
D. lacks capacity or ability to perform assigned tasks

11. The one of the following which is LEAST likely to be affected by improvements in the morale of personnel is employee   11.____

    A. skill   B. absenteeism
    C. turnover   D. job satisfaction

12. The one of the following situations in which it is LEAST appropriate for a supervisor to delegate authority to subordinates is where the supervisor   12.____

    A. lacks confidence in his own abilities to perform certain work
    B. is overburdened and cannot handle all his responsibilities
    C. refers all disciplinary problems to his subordinate
    D. has to deal with an emergency or crisis

13. Assume that it has come to your attention that two of your subordinates have shouted at each other and have almost engaged in a fist fight. Luckily, they were separated by some of the other employees.
Of the following, your BEST immediate course of action would *generally* be to   13.____

    A. reprimand the senior of the two subordinates since he should have known better
    B. hear the story from both employees and any witnesses and then take needed disciplinary action
    C. ignore the matter since nobody was physically hurt
    D. immediately suspend and fine both employees pending a departmental hearing

14. You have been delegating some of your authority to one of your subordinates because of his leadership potential. Which of the following actions is LEAST conducive to the growth and development of this individual for a supervisory position?   14.____

    A. Use praise only when it will be effective
    B. Give very detailed instructions and supervise the employee closely to be sure that the instructions are followed precisely
    C. Let the subordinate proceed with his planned course of action even if mistakes, within a permissible range, are made
    D. Intervene on behalf of the subordinate whenever an assignment becomes difficult for him

15. A rumor has been spreading in your department concerning the possibility of layoffs due to decreased revenues.
As a supervisor, you should GENERALLY   15.____

    A. deny the rumor, whether it is true or false, in order to keep morale from declining
    B. inform the men to the best of your knowledge about this situation and keep them advised of any new information
    C. tell the men to forget about the rumor and concentrate on increasing their productivity
    D. ignore the rumor since it is not authorized information

16. Within an organization, every supervisor should know to whom he reports and who reports to him.
    The one of the following which is achieved by use of such structured relationships is

    16.____

    A. unity of command
    B. confidentiality
    C. esprit de corps
    D. promotion opportunities

17. Almost every afternoon, one of your employees comes back from his break ten minutes late without giving you any explanation.
    Which of the following actions should you take FIRST in this situation?

    17.____

    A. Assign the employee to a different type of work and observe whether his behavior changes
    B. Give the employee extra work to do so that he will have to return on time
    C. Ask the employee for an explanation for his lateness
    D. Tell the employee he is jeopardizing the break for everyone

18. When giving instructions to your employees in a group, which one of the following should you make certain to do?

    18.____

    A. Speak in a casual, offhand manner
    B. Assume that your employees fully understand the instructions
    C. Write out your instructions beforehand and read them to the employees
    D. Tell exactly who is to do what

19. A fist fight develops between two men under your supervision.
    The MOST advisable course of action for you to take FIRST is to

    19.____

    A. call the police
    B. have the other workers pull them apart
    C. order them to stop
    D. step between the two men

20. You have assigned some difficult and unusual work to one of your most experienced and competent subordinates.
    If you notice that he is doing the work incorrectly, you should

    20.____

    A. assign the work to another employee
    B. reprimand him in private
    C. show him immediately how the work should be done
    D. wait until the job is completed and then correct his errors

KEY (CORRECT ANSWERS)

1.	D	11.	A
2.	D	12.	C
3.	D	13.	B
4.	B	14.	B
5.	A	15.	B
6.	C	16.	A
7.	D	17.	C
8.	B	18.	D
9.	A	19.	C
10.	B	20.	C

———

GLOSSARY OF TRAFFIC CONTROL TERMS

GLOSSARY OF TRAFFIC CONTROL TERMS

A

ACCESS ROAD - Public roads, existing or proposed, needed to provide essential access to military installation and facilities, or to industrial installations and facilities in the activities of which there is specific defense interest. Roads within the boundaries of military reservation are excluded from this definition unless such roads have been dedicated to public use and are not subject to closure.

ACCIDENT SPOT MAP - An area or installation map showing the location of vehicle accidents by means of symbols. Symbols may represent accidents classified as to daylight hours, night hours, injury or death.

ANGLE PARKING - Parking where the longitudinal axes of vehicles form an angle with the alignment of the roadway.

C

CENTER LINE - A line marking the center of a roadway between traffic moving in opposite direction.

COLLISION DIAGRAM - A plan of an intersection or section of roadway on which reported accidents are diagramed by means of arrows showing manner of collision.

COMBINED CONDITION AND COLLISION DIAGRAM - A condition diagram upon which the reported accidents are diagramed by means of arrows showing manner of collision.

CONDITION DIAGRAM - A plan of an intersection or section of roadway showing all objects and physical conditions having a bearing on traffic movement and safety at that location. Usually these are scaled drawings.

CORDON COUNTS - A count of all vehicles and persons entering and leaving a district (cordon area) during a designated period of time.

CORDON AREA - The district bounded by the cordon line and included in a cordon count.

CROSSWALK - Any portion of a roadway at an intersection or elsewhere distinctly indicated for pedestrian crossing by lines or other markings on the surface. Also, that part of a roadway at an intersection included within the connections of the lateral lines of the sidewalks on opposite sides of the trafficway measured from the curbs, or in the absence of curbs, from the edges of the traversable roadway.

D

DELAY - The time consumed while traffic or a specified component of traffic is impeded in its movement by some element over which it has no control usually expressed in seconds per vehicle.

DESIRE LINE - A straight line between the point of origin and point of destination of a trip without regard to routes of travel (used in connection with an origin-destination study).

DIVIDED STREET - A two-way road on which traffic in one direction of travel is separated from that in the opposite direction by a directional separator. Such a road has two or more roadways.

E

85 PERCENTILE SPEED - That speed below which 85 percent of the traffic units travel, and above which 15 percent travel.

F

FIXED-TIME CONTROLLER - An automatic controller for supervising the operation of traffic control signals in accordance with a predetermined fixed-time cycle and divisions thereof.

FIXED-TIME TRAFFIC SIGNAL - A traffic signal operated by a fixed-time controller.

FLASHING BEACON - A section of a standard traffic signal head, or a similar type device, having a yellow or red lens in each face, which is illuminated by rapid intermittent flashes.

FLASHING TRAFFIC SIGNAL - A traffic control signal used as a flashing beacon.

FLOATING CAR- An automobile driven in the traffic flow at the average speed of the surrounding vehicles.

FLOW DIAGRAM - The graphical representation of the traffic volumes on a road or street network or section thereof, showing by means of bands the relative volumes using each section of roadway during a given period of time, usually 1 hour.

H

HIGH FREQUENCY ACCIDENT LOCATION - A specific location where a large number of traffic accidents have occurred.

I

INTERSECTION APPROACH - That portion of an intersection leg which is used by traffic approaching the intersection.

L

LATERAL CLEARANCE - The distance between the edge of pavement and any lateral obstruction.

LATERAL OBSTRUCTION- Any fixed object located adjacent to the traveled way which reduces the transverse dimensions of the roadway.

LEFT TURN LANE - A lane within the normal surfaced width reserved for left turning vehicles.

M

MANUAL TRAFFIC CONTROL - The use of hand signals or manually operated devices by traffic control personnel to control traffic.

MANUAL COUNTER - A tallying device which is operated by hand.

MASS TRANSPORTATION - Movement of large groups of persons.

MULTIAXLE TRUCK - A truck which has more than two axles.

O

OCCUPANCY RATIO -The average number of occupants per vehicle (including the driver).

ODOMETER -A device on a vehicle for measuring the distance traveled, usually as a cumulative total, but sometimes also for individual trips, with an indicator on the instrument panel where it is usually combined with a speedometer indicator, or in the hub of a wheel in some trucks.

OFF-PEAK PERIOD - That portion of the day in which traffic volumes are relatively light.

OFFSET LANES - Additional lanes used for traffic which is heavier in one direction. Also known as unbalanced lanes.

OFF-STREET PARKING - Lots and garages intended for parking entirely off streets and alleys.

ON-STREET PARKING - The use of street and alleys (may be angle or parallel parking) for parking of vehicles.

ORIGIN DESTINATION STUDIES - A study of the origins and destinations of trips of vehicles and passengers. Usually included in the study are all trips within, or passing through, into or out of a selected area.

OVERALL SPEED - The total distance traversed divided by the travel time. Usually expressed in miles per hour and includes all delays.

OVERALL TIME - The time of travel, including stops and delays except those off the traveled way.

P

PARALLEL PARKING - Parking where the longitudinal axis of vehicles are parallel to alignment of the roadway so that the vehicles are facing in the same direction as the movement of adjacent vehicular traffic.

PARKING DURATION - Length of time a vehicle is parked.

PASSENGER VEHICLE - A free-wheeled, self-propelled vehicle designed for the transportation of persons but limited in seating capacity to not more than seven passengers, not including the driver. It includes taxicabs, limousines, and station wagons, but does not include motorcycles. (In capacity studies, also includes light reconnaissance vehicles, and pickup trucks.)

PASSENGER (TRANSIT) VOLUME - The total number of public transit occupants being transported in a period of time.

PEAK PERIOD - That portion of the day in which maximum traffic volumes are experienced.

PEDESTRIAN - Any person afoot. For purpose of accident classification, this will be interpreted to include any person riding in or upon a device moved or designed for movement by human power or the force of gravity, except bicycles, including stilts, skates, skis, sleds, toy wagons, and scooters.

PERCENT OF GRADE - The slope in the longitudinal direction of the pavement expressed in percent which is the number of units of change in elevation per 100 units of horizontal distance.

PERCENT OF GREEN TIME - The percentage of green time allotted to the direction of travel being studies.

PROPERTY DAMAGE - Damage to property as a result of a motor vehicle accident that may be a basis of a claim for compensation. Does not include compensation for loss of life or for personal injuries.

PUBLIC HIGHWAYS- The entire width between property lines, or boundary lines, of every way or place of which any part is open to use of the public for purposes of vehicular traffic as a matter of right or custom.

PUBLIC TRANSIT - The public passenger carrying service afforded by vehicles following regular routes and making specified stops.

R

REFLECTORIZE - The application of some material to traffic control devices or hazards which will return to the eyes of the road user some portion of the light from his vehicle headlights, thereby producing a brightness which attracts attention.

REGULATORY DEVICE - A device used to indicate the required method of traffic movement or use of the public trafficway.

REGULATORY SIGN - A sign used to indicate the required method of traffic movement or use of the traffic way.

RIGHT TURN LANE - A lane within the normal surfaced width reserved for right turning vehicles.

ROADWAY - That portion of a trafficway including shoulders, improved, designed, or ordinarily used for vehicle traffic.

S

SEPARATE TURNING LANE - Added traffic lane which is separated from the intersection area by an island or unpaved area. It may be wide enough for one- or two-lane operation.

SHOULDER - The portion of the roadway contiguous with the traveled way for accommodation of stopped vehicles, for emergency use, and for lateral support of base and surface courses.

SIGHT DISTANCES - The length of roadway visible to the driver of a passenger vehicle at any given point on the roadway when the view is unobstructed by traffic.

SIGNAL CYCLE - The total time required for one complete sequence of the intervals of a traffic signal.

SIGNAL CONTROLLER - A complete electrical mechanism for controlling the operation of traffic control signals, including the timer and all necessary auxiliary apparatus mounted in a cabinet.

SIGNAL FACE - That part of a signal head provided for controlling traffic from a single direction.

SIGNAL HEAD - An assembly containing one or more signal faces that may be designated accordingly as one-way, two-way, multi-way.

SIGNAL PHASE - A part of the total time cycle allocated to any traffic movements receiving the right-of-way or to any combination of traffic movements receiving the right-of-way simultaneously during one or more intervals

SIMPLE INTERSECTION - An intersection of two traffic ways, with four legs or approaches.

SPEED - The rate of movement of a vehicle, generally expressed in miles per hour.

STOPPING SIGHT DISTANCE - The distance required by a driver of a vehicle, traveling at a given speed, to bring his vehicle to a stop after an object on the roadway becomes visible.

STREET WIDTH - The width of the paved or traveled portion of the roadway.

T

THROUGH MOVEMENT - (See THROUGH TRAFFIC)

THROUGH STREET - A street on which traffic is given the right-of-way so that vehicles entering or crossing the street must yield the right-of-way.

THROUGH TRAFFIC - Traffic proceeding through a military installation or portion not originating in or destined to that military installation or portion thereof.

TIME CYCLE - (See SIGNAL CYCLE)

TRAFFIC - Pedestrians, **ridden or herd**ed animals, vehicles, street cars, and other conveyances, either singly or together, while using any street for purposes of travel.

TRAFFIC ACCIDENT - Any accident involving a motor vehicle in motion that results in death, injury, or property damage.

TRAFFIC ACTUATED CONTROLLER- An automatic controller for supervising the operation of traffic control signals in accordance with the immediate and varying demands of traffic as registered with the controller by means of detectors.

TRAFFIC CONTROL - All measures except those of a structural kind that serve to control and guide traffic and to promote road safety.

TRAFFIC CONTROL DEVICE - A Traffic control device is any sign, signal, marking, or device placed or erected for the purpose of regulating, warning, or guiding traffic.

TRAFFIC DEMAND - The volume of traffic desiring to use a particular route or facility.

TRAFFIC ENGINEERING - That phase of engineering that deals with the planning and geometric design of streets, highways, and abutting lands, and with traffic operations thereon, as their use is related to the safe, convenient, and economic transportation of persons and goods.

TRAFFIC FLOW - The movement of vehicles on a roadway.

TRAFFIC FLOW PATTERN - The distribution of traffic volumes on a street or highway network.

TRAFFIC GENERATOR - A traffic producing area such as a post exchange, parking lot, or administrative center.

TRAFFIC SIGNAL INTERVAL - Any one of the several divisions of the total time cycle during which signal indications do not change.

TRAFFICWAY - The entire width between property lines (or other boundary lines) of every way or place of which any part is open to use of public for purposes of vehicular traffic as a matter of right or custom. On military installation the word "public" refers to those persons having authorized access to, and use of, the common roadway facilities.

TRANSIT VEHICLE - A passenger carrying vehicle, such as a bus or street-car which follows regular routes and makes specific stops.

TRAVEL TIME- The total elapsed time from the origin to destination of a trip.

TURNING MOVEMENT - The traffic making a designated turn at an inter-section.

TWO-WAY STREETS - A street on which traffic may move in opposite directions simultaneously. It may be either divided or undivided.

TYPE OF ACCIDENT - The kind of motor vehicle accident, such as head-on, right-angle, etc.

TYPE OF SURFACE - The class of surface such as concrete, asphalt, gravel, etc.

U

UNINTERRRUPTED FLOW - The flow of vehicles under ideal conditions re-sulting in unrestricted movement.

V

VEHICLE - Every device in, upon, or by which any person or property is or may be transported or drawn upon a highway, except those devices moved by human power or used exclusively upon stationary rails or tracks.

VEHICULE OCCUPANCY - The average number of occupants per automobile, in-cluding the driver.

VOLUME - The number of vehicles passing a given point during a specified period of time.

W

WARNING SIGN - A sign used to indicate conditions that are actually or potentially hazardous to highway users.

WARRANT - Formally stated conditions that have been accepted as minimum requirements for justifying installation of a traffic control device or regulation.

ZONE (ORIGIN-DESTINATION STUDIES)$\underline{Z}$ - A division of an area established for the purpose of analyzing origin-destination studies. It may be bounded by physical barriers such as rivers and highways, or may be the location of individual work organizations that have duty stations in relatively close proximity.

———

ANSWER SHEET

TEST NO. ____________ PART ______ TITLE OF POSITION ____________________
(AS GIVEN IN EXAMINATION ANNOUNCEMENT - INCLUDE OPTION, IF ANY)

PLACE OF EXAMINATION ____________________ (CITY OR TOWN) ____________________ (STATE) DATE ____________

RATING

USE THE SPECIAL PENCIL. MAKE GLOSSY BLACK MARKS.

1	A B C D E	26	A B C D E	51	A B C D E	76	A B C D E	101	A B C D E
2	A B C D E	27	A B C D E	52	A B C D E	77	A B C D E	102	A B C D E
3	A B C D E	28	A B C D E	53	A B C D E	78	A B C D E	103	A B C D E
4	A B C D E	29	A B C D E	54	A B C D E	79	A B C D E	104	A B C D E
5	A B C D E	30	A B C D E	55	A B C D E	80	A B C D E	105	A B C D E
6	A B C D E	31	A B C D E	56	A B C D E	81	A B C D E	106	A B C D E
7	A B C D E	32	A B C D E	57	A B C D E	82	A B C D E	107	A B C D E
8	A B C D E	33	A B C D E	58	A B C D E	83	A B C D E	108	A B C D E
9	A B C D E	34	A B C D E	59	A B C D E	84	A B C D E	109	A B C D E
10	A B C D E	35	A B C D E	60	A B C D E	85	A B C D E	110	A B C D E

Make only ONE mark for each answer. Additional and stray marks may be counted as mistakes. In making corrections, erase errors COMPLETELY.

11	A B C D E	36	A B C D E	61	A B C D E	86	A B C D E	111	A B C D E
12	A B C D E	37	A B C D E	62	A B C D E	87	A B C D E	112	A B C D E
13	A B C D E	38	A B C D E	63	A B C D E	88	A B C D E	113	A B C D E
14	A B C D E	39	A B C D E	64	A B C D E	89	A B C D E	114	A B C D E
15	A B C D E	40	A B C D E	65	A B C D E	90	A B C D E	115	A B C D E
16	A B C D E	41	A B C D E	66	A B C D E	91	A B C D E	116	A B C D E
17	A B C D E	42	A B C D E	67	A B C D E	92	A B C D E	117	A B C D E
18	A B C D E	43	A B C D E	68	A B C D E	93	A B C D E	118	A B C D E
19	A B C D E	44	A B C D E	69	A B C D E	94	A B C D E	119	A B C D E
20	A B C D E	45	A B C D E	70	A B C D E	95	A B C D E	120	A B C D E
21	A B C D E	46	A B C D E	71	A B C D E	96	A B C D E	121	A B C D E
22	A B C D E	47	A B C D E	72	A B C D E	97	A B C D E	122	A B C D E
23	A B C D E	48	A B C D E	73	A B C D E	98	A B C D E	123	A B C D E
24	A B C D E	49	A B C D E	74	A B C D E	99	A B C D E	124	A B C D E
25	A B C D E	50	A B C D E	75	A B C D E	100	A B C D E	125	A B C D E

ANSWER SHEET

TEST NO. _____ PART _____ TITLE OF POSITION _____

(AS GIVEN IN EXAMINATION ANNOUNCEMENT - INCLUDE OPTION, IF ANY)

PLACE OF EXAMINATION _____ DATE_____

(CITY OR TOWN)   (STATE)

RATING

USE THE SPECIAL PENCIL. MAKE GLOSSY BLACK MARKS.

Answer grid, questions 1–10, columns with options A B C D E:

1   26   51   76   101
2   27   52   77   102
3   28   53   78   103
4   29   54   79   104
5   30   55   80   105
6   31   56   81   106
7   32   57   82   107
8   33   58   83   108
9   34   59   84   109
10 35   60   85   110

Make only ONE mark for each answer. Additional and stray marks may be
counted as mistakes. In making corrections, erase errors COMPLETELY.

Answer grid, questions 11–25, columns with options A B C D E:

11   36   61   86   111
12   37   62   87   112
13   38   63   88   113
14   39   64   89   114
15   40   65   90   115
16   41   66   91   116
17   42   67   92   117
18   43   68   93   118
19   44   69   94   119
20   45   70   95   120
21   46   71   96   121
22   47   72   97   122
23   48   73   98   123
24   49   74   99   124
25   50   75   100 125